Fundamentals of Pure and Applied Economics 23
Editors-in-Chief: Jacques Lesourne and Hugo Sonnenschein

Disequilibrium Trade Theories

Motoshige Itoh and
Takashi Negishi

harwood academic publishers

Disequilibrium Trade Theories

Continued on inside back cover

Disequilibrium Trade Theories

Motoshige Itoh

and

Takashi Negishi
University of Tokyo, Japan

A volume in the International Trade section
edited by
Murray Kemp
University of New South Wales, Australia

harwood academic publishers
chur · london · paris · new york · melbourne

© 1987 by Harwood Academic Publishers GmbH
Poststrasse 22, 7000 Chur, Switzerland
All rights reserved

Harwood Academic Publishers

Post Office Box 197
London WC2E 9PX
England

58, rue Lhomond
75005 Paris
France

Post Office Box 786
Cooper Station
New York, NY 10276
United States of America

Camberwell Business Center
Private Bag 30
Camberwell, Victoria 3124
Australia

Library of Congress Cataloging-in-Publication Data

Itoh, Motoshige, 1951–
    Disequilibrium trade theories.

    (Fundamentals of pure and applied economics,
vol. 23. International trade section, ISSN 0191-1708)
    Bibliography: p.
    Includes index.
    1. Commerce.   2. Equilibrium (Economics)
I. Takashi, Negishi, 1933–   . II. Title.
III. Series: Fundamentals of pure and applied
economics; vol. 23.   IV. Series: Fundamentals of
pure and applied economics. International trade
section.
HF1008.I86   1987   380.1   87-11834
ISBN 3-7186-0412-4

3 2280 00752 1982

Contents

Introduction to the Series

Drawing on a personal network, an economist can still relatively easily stay well informed in the narrow field in which he works, but to keep up with the development of economics as a whole is a much more formidable challenge. Economists are confronted with difficulties associated with the rapid development of their discipline. There is a risk of "balkanisation" in economics, which may not be favorable to its development.

Fundamentals of Pure and Applied Economics has been created to meet this problem. The discipline of economics has been subdivided into sections (listed inside). These sections include short books, each surveying the state of the art in a given area.

Each book starts with the basic elements and goes as far as the most advanced results. Each should be useful to professors needing material for lectures, to graduate students looking for a global view of a particular subject, to professional economists wishing to keep up with the development of their science, and to researchers seeking convenient information on questions that incidentally appear in their work.

Each book is thus a presentation of the state of the art in a particular field rather than a step-by-step analysis of the development of the literature. Each is a high-level presentation but accessible to anyone with a solid background in economics, whether engaged in business, government, international organizations, teaching, or research in related fields.

Three aspects of *Fundamentals of Pure and Applied Economics* should be emphasized:

—First, the project covers the whole field of economics, not only theoretical or mathematical economics.

—Second, the project is open-ended and the number of books is not predetermined. If new interesting areas appear, they will generate additional books.

—Last, all the books making up each section will later be grouped to constitute one or several volumes of an Encyclopedia of Economics.

The editors of the sections are outstanding economists who have selected as authors for the series some of the finest specialists in the world.

J. Lesourne   *H. Sonnenschein*

Disequilibrium Trade Theories

MOTOSHIGE ITOH and TAKASHI NEGISHI
University of Tokyo, Japan

INTRODUCTION

All happy families resemble one another, but each unhappy family is unhappy in its own way (Tolstoy). Equilibrium international trade theory belongs to a very homogeneous system of equilibrium economic theories developed by happy neo-classical economists who believe in the smooth functioning of the price mechanism in a free market society. Disequilibrium international trade theories are, however, quite heterogeneous, depending on related or corresponding different anti-neo-classical economic theories insisted on by unhappy economists who do not believe in the functioning of the price mechanism.

Among such anti-neo-classical theories, two theories are most important and most influential, i.e., neo-Ricardian or neo-Marxian theory ([41], [82]) and Keynesian theory. In the neo-Ricardian and neo-Marxian theories, real wages are given exogenously, i.e., by physiological, social and historical factors in neo-Ricardian and neo-Marxian theories, so that generally the labor market does not clear unless the Malthusian law of population works instantaneously. Keynesian economists assume that money wages are independent of the existence of the excess supply of labor: or, at least, they do not believe that the labor market is quickly cleared by changes in money wages. The disequilibrium trade theories to be surveyed below are, in a sense, related either to exogenously given real wages or to sticky money wages.

First, the problems of the so-called minimum wage economy are considered (in Sections one through three), where the labor market

---

The authors are grateful to Professor M. C. Kemp, who kindly read the early manuscript and suggested many improvements.

is subject to a wage floor which is exogenously given in real terms. The minimum real wage is considered to be set by some institutional arrangement such as custom, unions or law, and treated as a fact of life which, for social or political reasons, government and unions are unable or unwilling to alter ([3]). It will be shown that the introduction of the minimum real wage generates many interesting unorthodox results concerning unemployment, the terms of trade, gains from trade, international capital movements. We may emphasize, however, that these results are obtained by the use of theoretical tools developed in the neo-classical theory of international trade. The neo-classical economic theory can successfully be applied, with some necessary modifications, to the case of real wages exogenously given, whose importance has been insisted on by neo-Ricardian and neo-Marxian economists.

Keynesian economics with unchanged money wages and unemployment has recently been generalized to fix-price economics in which the prices of goods as well as wages are fixed in terms of money, independently of the existence of excess demand or supply in the goods and labor markets. The second problem we shall consider below is the application of the fix-price model to international trade (Sections four through seven). While some interesting results are available on unemployment, balance of payments, etc., our discussion will also reveal that important problems still remaining to be solved in this generalized Keynesian theory, i.e., in fix-price and quantity constraint models.

1. THE STRUCTURE OF MINIMUM-WAGE ECONOMIES

In this section we present simple models of minimum-wage economies and examine their production structure: we investigate how the patterns of production, consumption and trade are determined by commodity prices and the form of wage-rigidity. Although the way resources are allocated among industries depends on underlying production technology and the type of factor-price rigidity, minimum-wage economies, in general, share a common property that the slope of the transformation curve (marginal rate of transformation in production) is not equal to relative commodity price. This distortion, which is a result of the existence of unemployed factors of production, is the basic reason why minimum-wage economies have many special features that an undistorted economy does not have.

1.1. The basic model: specific-factors model with real wage rigidity

We first present a simple model, which will be used repeatedly in this paper to illustrate various results in their simplest forms. Consider the standard two-good model with three factors of production as follows:[1]

$$X_1 = F(L_1, K_1) \tag{1.1}$$

$$X_2 = G(L_2, K_2), \tag{1.2}$$

where K_1 and K_2 are, respectively, specific factors of production in sectors 1 and 2, which we call capital, and L_1 and L_2 are the amount of labor inputs in sector 1 and sector 2. Labor is assumed to be mobile between the two sectors. We assume that labor and the two types of capital are inelastically supplied. Denote by $\bar{L}$ the amount of labor supply. We then have

$$L_1 + L_2 = \bar{L}. \tag{1.3}$$

We call this model a specific-factors model.

Note that explicit consideration of capital is not necessary for the analysis in the present section and for the most part in the following sections. This particular formulation is adopted for convenience of dealing with the problem of industrial adjustment and that of capital movement, both of which will be discussed in the next section. One may assume production functions with labor the only explicitly considered factor of production and with decreasing marginal productivity of labor.

We assume that factor prices of the two types of capital are flexible while the factor price of labor, called the wage, is downward rigid. More specifically, we assume that the wage rate measured in units of good 2 has a minimum floor and the wage rate does not fall below the minimum floor level. This formulation of wage-rigidity is only for simple exposition. Other types of wage-rigidity will be introduced in Section 1.2.

---

[1] See Caves and Jones [33] for the structure of this model.

Several alternative reasons can be found for the downward rigidity of the real wage. The real wage may be indexed institutionally. The theory of the efficient wage, as expounded by Shapiro and Stiglitz [80], Weiss [89] and Yellen [91], provides a mechanism under which the real wage becomes downward rigid.

Figure 1 illustrates the allocation of labor between the two industries. On the vertical axis are plotted the values of the marginal product of labor in the two sectors measured in units of good 2, while on the horizontal axis are plotted the amounts of labor inputs in the two sectors, where the labor input in sector 1 is measured from the point 0_1 to the right and that in sector 2 is measured from the point 0_2 to the left. The curves A_1A_1 and A_2A_2 depict respectively the relation between the value of the marginal product of labor and the amount of labor input in sectors 1 and 2. The length of the line segment 0_10_2 represents the total labor supply of the economy, $\bar{L}$.

When the real wage rate in units of good 2 has a minimum-floor w_0, depicted on the vertical axis of the figure, L_1 units of labor will

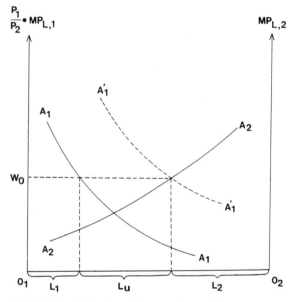

FIGURE 1   Allocation of labor under a minimum-wage.

be employed in sector 1, L_2 units of labor will be employed in sector 2, and L_u units of labor will become unemployed. (All of these are depicted on the horizontal axis of the figure.) Obviously, the amount of labor employed in each sector is determined by the level of the minimum-wage as well as by the relative price of the two goods. The higher is the minimum-wage level, the smaller is the amount of labor employed in each sector, and therefore the larger is the amount of unemployed labor. The amount of unemployed labor, under a given minimum-wage level, becomes smaller as the relative price of good 1 measured in units of good 2 becomes higher. A rise in the relative price of good 1 causes an upward shift of the curve A_1A_1 in Figure 1. The labor input in sector 1 increases while that in sector 2 does not change. Note also that when the relative price of good 1 is higher than the level indicated by the curve $A_1'A_1'$, the minimum-wage is no longer binding and labor will be fully employed.

The transformation curve of this economy has a shape like that of the curve FEB in Figure 2. The minimum-wage constraint is binding on the portion EF. As the relative price of good 1 rises, the production point moves to the right on the line segment EF, and

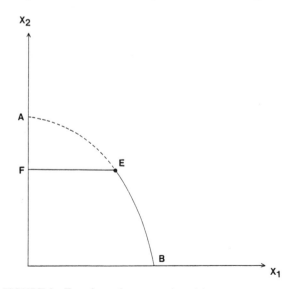

FIGURE 2 Transformation curve of a minimum-wage economy.

the employment and output of sector 1 increases while the output of sector 2 does not change. On the portion EB the real wage rate in units of good 2 is higher than the minimum-wage level, and therefore the minimum-wage constraint is not binding.

1.2. Some other forms of wage-rigidity

The simple model presented above can be used to consider other types of wage rigidity. In the present section we consider two types of wage rigidity which often appear in the trade literature: one is the case where wage restriction is specified by the so called wage function, and the other is the Harris–Todaro model.

Consider first the case where the minimum-wage level is given by the following wage function

$$w = H(p_1, p_2) \qquad (1.4)$$

where w is a nominal wage rate, and p_1 and p_2 are the nominal prices of goods 1 and 2. Since our main concern in this section is real wage rigidity, we assume that there is no money illusion. The wage function then becomes linear homogeneous in p_1 and p_2 whose partial derivative with respect to each price is non-negative. Note that the wage-rigidity considered in the previous section is a special case of this wage function, where the partial derivative with respect to p_1 is zero.

When the wage function is linear homogeneous, the real wage rate in units of good 2, w/p_2 can be written as

$$w/p_2 = H(p_1/p_2, 1) \qquad (1.5)$$

Therefore, the allocation of labor between the two sectors under the wage function is essentially the same as the one in the previous section with only minor modification: that is, w_0 in Figure 1 is replaced by $H(p_1/p_2, 1)$.

The amount of labor employed in each sector is determined as satisfying the following conditions as long as the minimum-wage constraint specified by the wage function is binding.

$$(p_1/p_2)MP_{L,1} = H(p_1/p_2, 1) \qquad (1.6)$$

$$MP_{L,2} = H(p_1/p_2, 1) \qquad (1.7)$$

where $MP_{L,1}$ $(i = 1, 2)$ is the physical marginal productivity of labor in sector i. By differentiating (1.6) and (1.7) logarithmically, we obtain

$$\hat{L}_1 = \{(1 - \lambda)/\varepsilon_1\}(\hat{p}_1 - \hat{p}_2) \tag{1.8}$$

$$\hat{L}_2 = -(\lambda/\varepsilon_2)(\hat{p}_1 - \hat{p}_2) \tag{1.9}$$

where

$$\lambda = \frac{\partial H}{\partial p_1} \cdot \frac{p_1}{w}$$

$$\varepsilon_i = -\frac{dML_{L,i}}{dL_i} \frac{L_i}{MP_{L,i}} \qquad (i = 1, 2)$$

λ is the elasticity of $H(p_1/p_2, 1)$ with respect to the relative price p_1/p_2, which can be interpreted as the share of consumption expenditure on good 1, ε_1 and ε_2 are the elasticity of the marginal productivity of labor with respect to labor input in the two sectors, and the hat symbol "^" above each variable indicates the rate of change of the variable. (1.8) and (1.9) state that a rise in the relative price of good 1 increases the amount of labor employed in sector 1 and decreases that in sector 2.

The total amount of labor employed changes as satisfying

$$\hat{L} = \theta_1 \hat{L}_1 + \theta_2 \hat{L}_2 = \{(1 - \lambda)\theta_1/\varepsilon_1 - \lambda\theta_2/\varepsilon_2\}(\hat{p}_1 - \hat{p}_2) \tag{1.10}$$

as long as the minimum-wage constraint is binding, where

$$\theta_1 = L_1/L, \qquad \theta_2 = L_2/L = 1 - \theta_1.$$

Therefore, the total amount of labor employed L and the relative price p_1/p_2 move in the same direction if and only if

$$(1 - \lambda)\theta_1/\varepsilon_1 > \lambda\theta_2/\varepsilon_2.$$

We cannot make any general statement about the direction of the change in L, but if the elasticities ε_1, ε_2 and λ are constant, then there is a critical level $(p_1/p_2)^*$ of the relative price at which the amount of labor employed is the smallest, and the relative price p_1/p_2 and the amount of labor employed move in the same direction if and only if the relative price is higher than this critical level.

Although the relation between the amount of labor employed and the relative commodity price in the present case is different from the case previously considered, the two cases share two common properties that play an important role in the following sections: that is, the slope of the transformation curve, namely the marginal rate of transformation in production, is not generally equal to the relative commodity price, and the amount of labor employed changes with the relative commodity price.

Let us next explain the Harris–Todaro model briefly.[2] The economy consists of the rural sector (sector 1) and the urban sector (sector 2). The producer's wage in sector 2, namely the real wage rate in sector 2 measured in units of good 2, is downward rigid at some level, say w_0. The real wage in the rural sector is determined as satisfying the following condition:

$$w = (p_1/p_2)MP_{L,1} = w_0 L_2/(\bar{L} - L_1), \qquad (1.11)$$

where w is the real wage rate in the rural sector measured in units of good 2.

The term $L_2/(\bar{L} - L_1)$ indicates the probability of being employed when a rural worker moves to the urban sector: $\bar{L} - L_1$ is the total labor supply to the urban sector, and L_2 is the amount of labor demand in the urban sector. Note that all workers not employed in the rural sector are assumed to move to the urban sector. The rural workers are paid their values of marginal product, while the workers employed in the urban sector are paid the amount $p_2 w_0$ in the nominal unit. It is assumed that the wage rate is higher in the urban sector than in the rural sector. Otherwise, labor is fully employed. For the workers in the rural sector there are two alternatives: one is to remain in the rural sector and earn the low wage, and the other is to move to the urban sector and look for a highly-paid job. The chance that the workers find jobs in the urban sector is given by the ratio of the total labor demand in the urban sector to the total labor supply in that sector. The expected real wage in the urban sector is the product of the probability of being employed and the wage rate w_0. Labor is then allocated between the two sectors so that the real wage rate in the rural sector is equal to the expected real wage rate in the urban sector.

---

[2] See Bhagwati and Srinivasan [28] and Harris and Todaro [44] for the detail of this model.

Note that the essential structure of the Harris–Todaro model is the same as the simple model previously considered. Figure 3 illustrates the allocation of labor in this economy. w_0 is an exogenously given urban wage, and L_2 is the amount of labor employed in the sector. L_1 is the amount of labor employed in the rural sector, and the wage rate in the rural sector is equal to $\{L_2/(\bar{L} - L_1)\}w_0$. L_3 indicates the amount of unemployed labor.

1.3. More general characterization of minimum-wage economies

Although the analysis we have presented so far is enough for our discussion in the following sections, it might be useful to summarize the basic characters of minimum-wage economies in the framework of a many-good, many-factor model.

Consider an economy with n goods and $(m + m^*)$ factors of production. Each good is assumed to be produced under a production function

$$X_i = F^i(K_1^i, \ldots, K_m^i; L_1^i, \ldots, L_{m^*}^i), \qquad (i = 1, 2, \ldots, n),$$

where X_i is the output of good i, $K_1^i, \ldots, K_m^i; L_1^i, \ldots, L_{m^*}^i$ are the $(m + m^*)$ factors of production used for the production of good i,

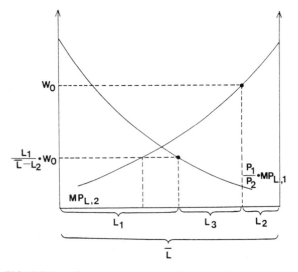

FIGURE 3 Allocation of labor in a Harris–Todaro economy.

and $F^i(\ldots;\ldots)$ is a neoclassical, linear homogeneous production function. Although we restrict our analysis to the case of non-joint production and no input of intermediate goods, extension of the analysis to more general cases is possible.[3]

m factors of production $K_1, \ldots, K_m$ are flexible-price factors of production, whose factor-prices move freely so as to satisfy full employment conditions for these factors. We denote by $r_1, \ldots, r_m$ these factor prices. m^* factors of production $L_1, \ldots, L_{m^*}$ are fix-price factors of production: their factor prices, denoted by $w_1, \ldots, w_{m^*}$, are downward rigid, and the levels of these minimum floors are so high relative to commodity prices (denoted by $p_1, \ldots, p_n$) that some portion of each factor is not used for production.

Note that the structure of the present model is essentially the same as a model with m^* factors internationally freely mobile under a given set of factor prices (small country assumption in the world factor market). In the former case some portion of each factor is not used for production, while in the latter case that part is used for the production in the rest of the world through international factor movements. Although the national income level is higher in the latter by the amount of factor rewards from the rest of the world, the domestic output level of each industry is exactly the same in the two cases.

Under the above setting, the relative size of n (the number of goods) and m (the number of flexible-price factors) become important to determine the nature of equilibrium just in the same manner as in the usual neoclassical trade models with many goods and many factors. When n is larger than m, the country does not produce all goods except in special cases. When n is smaller than m, the economy generally produces all goods unless prices of some goods are extremely high or low.

Consider first the case where n is larger than m. From the production function we can derive so called unit cost functions[4]

$$c^i(r_1, \ldots, r_m; w_1, \ldots, w_{m^*})$$
$$= \left\{ \min \sum_{j=1}^{m} r_j K_j^i + \sum_{j=1}^{m^*} w_j L_j^i : \text{s.t. } F^i(K^i, L^i) \geq 1 \right\}$$

---

[3] See Neary [71].
[4] See Dixit and Norman [39] and Mussa [69] for the concept of the unit cost function.

where
$$K^i = (K^i_1, \ldots, K^i_m), \qquad L^i = (L^i_1, \ldots, L^i_{m^*}).$$

Using this unit cost function, factor market equilibrium under given commodity prices $p_1, \ldots, p_n$ and given fixed factor-prices $w_1, \ldots, w_{m^*}$ can be expressed by the following equations:

$$p_i \lessgtr c^i(r, w) \qquad i = 1, 2, \ldots, n,$$

where
$$r = (r_1, \ldots, r_m), \qquad w = (w_1, \ldots, w_{m^*}).$$

Good i is produced only when the above condition is satisfied with equality for good i.

It is obvious that the economy will specialize in the production of at most m goods except under special set of prices. Figure 4 illustrates the above point in the case of two goods, one flexible-price factor (called capital) and one fix-price factor (called labor). This case is discussed by Brecher [2, 3].

The curves 11 and 22 denote respectively the values of r and w satisfying:

$$p_1 = c^1(r, w)$$
$$p_2 = c^2(r, w),$$

FIGURE 4   Factor-price frontiers and a minimum-wage.

for given prices of the two goods, p_1 and p_2, where w and r are the factor prices of labor and capital. When the wage is downward rigid at the level w_0 as shown in the figure, sector 1 can provide a higher rental on capital than sector 2 under the given set of prices. Therefore, the economy will specialize in the production of good 1 in this case.

Although the economy in general specializes in the production of a subset of goods when the number of flexible-price factors of production is smaller than the number of goods, there are particular prices under which the economy produces all good, and this case attracted much attention of theoretical analysis. There is a reason why this case attracted attention.

In Figure 4 this case is illustrated by the situation where the price of good 1 is at such a level that the factor-price frontier of sector 1 goes through the point E. (The dotted curve $1'1'$ in the figure depicts the factor price frontier of sector 1 under this price.) In this case the economy will produce two goods even if the wage level is downward rigid at w_0. Given the factor-prices w_0 and r_0 as shown in the figure, the factor input coefficients a_{li} and a_{ki} ($i = 1, 2$) are given so as to minimize the unit costs of the two sectors, where a_{li} and a_{ki} are the amount of labor and capital required for unit output of good i.

The total demand for labor and capital in this economy are then given as functions of the outputs of the two goods:

$$L^d = a_{l1}X_1 + a_{l2}X_2$$
$$K^d = a_{k1}X_1 + a_{k2}X_2,$$

where $a_{l1}X_1$ and $a_{l2}X_2$ are the total labor inputs in sectors 1 and 2 when the outputs of these two sectors are X_1 and X_2, and $a_{k1}X_1$ and $a_{k2}X_2$ are the total capital inputs in the two sectors. Thus, in the space of X_1 and X_2 depicted in Figure 5, we can draw iso-labor-employment lines and iso-capital-employment lines. (We do not draw these lines in the figure.) The iso-labor-employment lines have a common slope—a_{l1}/a_{l2}, and a higher employment level corresponds to a line located in the north-east. Similarly, iso-capital-employment lines have a common slope—a_{k1}/a_{k2}.

The lines A_1A_2 and B_1B_2 in Figure 5 illustrate the iso-labor-employment line and iso-capital-employment line for the levels of $\bar{L}$

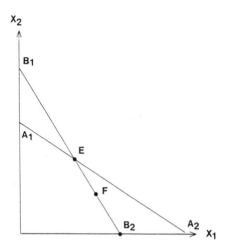

FIGURE 5 Rybczynski lines and a minimum-wage.

and $\bar{K}$, where $\bar{L}$ and $\bar{K}$ are the endowments of labor and capital of this economy. (Since these lines are often called "Rybczynski lines", we use this terminology in the following.) Since the factor-price of capital is flexible and capital is fully utilized, the pair of the outputs of the two goods must be located on the line B_1B_2 (Rybczynski line of capital). On the other hand there is no reason why labor should be fully employed, since the wage is downward rigid.

In the case illustrated in Figure 5, any point on the line segment EB_2 can be an equilibrium under this particular set of commodity prices. Suppose, for example, that this economy is not trading with the rest of the world and that the demand of this economy can be represented by a homothetic utility function. Furthermore, suppose that at the point F in the figure the slope of an indifference curve is equal to minus the relative price. Then, the point F becomes the autarkic equilibrium point of this economy under the downward rigid wage, and some labor will be unemployed. There is no mechanism under which this unemployed labor becomes employed unless the wage rate falls.

In the general case of n-goods we can derive a similar linear portion of the transformation curve at which the economy does not specialize in production. Suppose that the number of goods n is larger than the number of flexible-price factors of production m.

Given m^* fix-factor prices $w_1, \ldots, w_{m^*}$, the production equilibrium of this economy is given by

$$p_i \leqq c^i(r, w).$$

We can choose the set of prices such that the above conditions are satisfied with equality for more than m goods.

Suppose, for example, that the equality conditions are satisfied for the first $\bar{n}$ goods, where $m < \bar{n} \leqq n$. Then, the demand for each factor of production can be written as

$$K_j^d = \sum_{i=1}^{\bar{n}} a_{kj}^i X_i \qquad j = 1, 2, \ldots, m$$

$$L_h^d = \sum_{i=1}^{\bar{n}} a_{lh}^i X_i \qquad h = 1, 2, \ldots, m^*$$

where K_j^d and L_h^d are the demand for factor K_j (flexible-price factor) and for factor L_h (fix-price factor), X_i is the output of good i, and

$$a_{kj}^i = \frac{\partial c^i(r; w)}{\partial r_j}, \qquad a_{lh}^i = \frac{\partial c^i(r; w)}{\partial w_h}.$$

a_{kj}^i and a_{lh}^i are the input levels of the factors K_j and L_h for a unit production of good i. We assume that the cost functions $c^i(.;.)$ have full dimensionality in the sense that the Jacobian matrix of the partial derivatives of the m cost functions with respect to n flexible factor prices $r_1, \ldots, r_n$ has dimension of m. (Thus, under given prices of commodities and fix-price factors, the prices of flexible-price factors are determined uniquely and independently of factor endowments.)

We can now proceed as for the two-good case. All of the m flexible-price factors are fully employed; therefore

$$\bar{K}_j = \sum_{i=1}^{\bar{n}} a_{kj}^i X_i \qquad j = 1, 2, \ldots, m$$

is satisfied, where $\bar{K}_j$ is the endowment of K_j factor.

Note that there are $\bar{n}$ endogenous variables $X_1, X_2, \ldots, X_{\bar{n}}$, while there are only m equations. Thus, the variables $X_1, X_2, \ldots, X_n$ can move on the set

$$\left\{ (X_1, X_2, \ldots, X_{\bar{n}}) \in R^{\bar{n}} : X_i \geqq 0, \ \sum_{i=1}^{\bar{n}} a_{kj}^i X_i = \bar{K}_j, \ \sum_{i=1}^{\bar{n}} a_{lh}^i X_i \leqq \bar{L}_h \right\},$$

where $\bar{L}_h$ is the endowment of the factor L_h. In general this set has $(\bar{n} - m)$ dimensions. Thus, corresponding to one particular set of prices satisfying equality conditions for $\bar{n}$ commodities, there is a $(\bar{n} - m)$ dimensional linear set of production of these $\bar{n}$ commodities.

Needless to say, the national income level changes as one moves along this linear set. Since the national income level is given by

$$\sum_{i=1}^{\bar{n}} p_i X_i = \sum_{j=1}^{m} r_j \bar{K}_j + \sum_{h=1}^{m^*} w_h L_h,$$

where L_h is the amount of the factor L_h actually employed. As one moves along the linear set, L_h $(h = 1, \ldots, m^*)$ changes and therefore the national income level also changes. As we explain in the next section, various unorthodox results can be derived in a minimum-wage economy because of this change in the national income. Note that, in Figure 5, the amount of employment increases as one moves along EB_2 in the direction of E.

Another important fact, which also becomes a cause of various unusual features of minimum-wage economy, is that the slope of this linear portion is not equal to the relative price of goods corresponding to this flat portion. For example, in Figure 5, the slope of the line segment is $-a_{k1}/a_{k2}$, which is larger in absolute value than the relative price p_1/p_2.[5]

The flat portion we discussed above has attracted some attention in the literature, since the possibility that the equilibrium production point is located on this linear segment cannot be neglected and may be perhaps quite large under certain circumstances. It might be useful to explain why the possibility cannot be neglected. We again use the simple two-good case due to Brecher [2, 3].

Suppose that the real wage rate measured in units of good 2 is downward rigid. Figure 6 depicts the factor-price frontiers of sector 1 (the curve $A_1 A_2$) and sector 2 (the curve $B_1 B_2$), where the wage rate in the unit of good 2 is plotted on the vertical axis and the capital-rental also measured in the unit of good 2 is plotted on the horizontal axis. Each point on the factor-price frontier corresponds to a different capital-labor input ratio. As one moves downward

---

[5] It is easy to show that the relative price p_1/p_2 is smaller than a_{k1}/a_{k2} but larger than a_{12}/a_{12}.

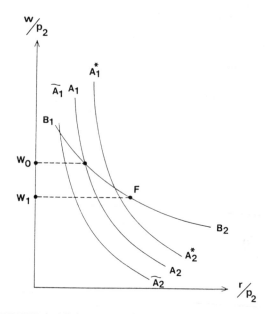

FIGURE 6   Minimum-wage level and specialization pattern.

along the factor-price frontier, one has a lower capital-labor input ratio. In fact, the slope of the frontier at each point is equal to the capital-labor input ratio chosen by the producers under the factor-prices given by the point.[6] The location of the factor-price frontier of good 1 moves with the relative price p_1/p_2: a rise in the relative price shifts the frontier to the north-east.

The structure of this minimum-wage economy becomes slightly different depending on whether the minimum-wage level is above or below a critical level, where the critical level depends on the capital-labor endowment ratio. Let the point F in Figure 6 be the one at which the slope of the factor-price frontier of the second industry is equal to minus the capital-labor endowment ratio (denoted by $\bar{k}$). w_1 plotted on the vertical axis of the figure is the critical wage level mentioned above. When the minimum-wage level is below this level, then the equilibrium point at which the economy

---

[6] See Dixit and Norman [39] and Mussa [69] for the concept of the factor price frontier.

produces both goods carries the character illustrated by Figure 5: that is, the two Rybczynski lines intersect in the positive orthant and there is a possibility that labor is fully employed. In the following we restrict our analysis to the case where the minimum-wage is above the critical level. (Thus, labor is not fully employed as long as both goods are produced.) However, a similar analysis can be made for the case where the minimum-wage is below the critical level.

Suppose that the minimum-wage is at the level w_0 shown in Figure 6. Then, three different production patterns can arise.

When the relative price of the two goods is at such a level that the factor-price frontier of sector 1 is located at the position as the curve A_1A_2 in Figure 6, then the economy will engage in the production of both goods. In this case both sectors can provide the same capital rental r_0 under the minimum-wage w_0. The capital-labor input ratios of the two sectors under this relative price are given by the slope of the factor-price frontiers of the two sectors at the point E_0. Denote by k_1 and k_2 these capital-labor input ratios at this point. We have

$$k_1 > k_2 > k_0,$$

where k_0 is the capital-labor endowment ratio. We assume that sector 1 is a capital-intensive sector. The second inequality is due to our assumption that the minimum-wage is above the critical wage level w_1 and labor is not fully employed in this case. In other words, the minimum wage level is so high that the capital-labor input ratios of the two sectors become extremely high as compared with the capital-labor endowment ratio.

The line segment AB in Figure 7 illustrates the output levels of the two goods achieved under the price ratio. This line segment is nothing but the capital Rybczynski line which we have already explained in Figure 5. (The labor Rybczynski line is located to the north-east of AB and the two lines do not intersect in the positive orthant.) As more capital moves from labor-intensive sector 2 to capital-intensive sector 1, the production point moves from A to B along this line segment. There is more unemployed labor as one moves along the line segment from A to B.

When the relative price of good 1 in terms of good 2 is lower than the level under which the economy produces both goods, the

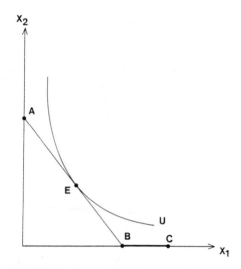

FIGURE 7   A case of incomplete specialization.

economy will specialize in the production of good 2. In this case the factor-price frontier of sector 1 is located at positions like that of $\bar{A}_1 \bar{A}_2$ in Figure 6. Under the minimum-wage w_0 sector 2 can provide a higher capital rental than sector 1, and therefore all capital is absorbed by sector 2. Note that in this case the capital-labor input ratio of sector 2 is always equal to the slope of the factor-price frontier of the sector at E_0 and its does not change with the relative price. Thus, the output of good 2 as well as the employment level do not move as long as the relative price stays in this region. The point A in Figure 7 illustrates the output of the economy in this case.

When the relative price of good 1 in units of good 2 is higher than the level under which the economy produces both goods, the economy will specialize in the production of good 1. In this case the factor-price frontier of sector 1 is located at a position like the curve $A_1^* A_2^*$ in Figure 6. Under the minimum wage w_0 sector 1 can provide a higher capital rental than sector 2. Thus, all capital is absorbed in sector 1. Note that the capital-labor input ratio of sector 1 falls as the relative price of good 1 rises. Thus, the producers in sector 1 will use capital more intensively as the relative price of good 1 rises.

The portion BC in Figure 7 illustrates the production points when the economy specializes in the production of good 1. As the relative price of good 1 rises, the production point moves toward C along the line segment BC. Once the relative price becomes high enough, the minimum-wage is no longer binding. Thus, full employment is achieved at C.

It is obvious from Figure 7 that there is quite a possibility that the economy produces both goods. For example, suppose that demand is represented by indifference curves which do not intersect with the two axes. Then, the autarkic equilibrium of the economy becomes the point at which the slope of an indifference curve is equal to the slope of the line segment AB. The point E in Figure 7 illustrates the autarkic equilibrium, where U is an indifference curve.

In order to examine the nature of trade equilibrium, it is useful to derive the offer curve of this economy. If we assume that demand is represented by normally shaped indifference curves of the representative individual, the offer curve has a shape like that of the curve $QA0BQ'$ in Figure 8, where the export of good 1 by the country is plotted on the horizontal axis and the import of good 2 is plotted on the vertical axis. Ths points A, 0 and B on this curve correspond respectively to the points A, E and B on the transformation curve in Figure 7. $Q*0Q*'$ illustrates the offer curve of the rest of the world. The figure is drawn in such a way that the two offer curves intersect on the flat portion AB of the home country's

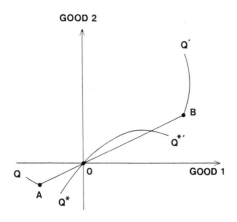

FIGURE 8 Trade equilibrium of a minimum-wage economy.

offer curve. In this case the home country produces both goods under free trade equilibrium. It is now obvious that there is a substantial possibility that the economy produces both goods even under trade equilibrium.

Let us return to our original general case. When the number of goods n is smaller than the number of flexible-price factors of production m, the economy will generally produce all goods and there is no flat portion like the one discussed above. However, even in this case the slope of the transformation curve is not equal to the relative commodity prices.

It is not difficult to see that the slope of the transformation curve is not equal to relative commodity prices under rigid factor-prices. In general the changes in output of good i (dX_i) can be expressed as

$$dX_i = \sum_{j=1}^{m} F_j^i \, dK_j^i + \sum_{h=1}^{m^*} F_h^i \, dL_h^i$$

$$= \left(\sum_{j=1}^{m} r_j \, dK_j^i + \sum_{h=1}^{m^*} dL_h^i \right) \Big/ p_i$$

We thus have

$$\frac{d(\sum_{i=2}^{n} p_i X_i)}{dX_1} = P_1 \cdot \frac{\sum_{j=1}^{m} r_j (\sum_{i=2}^{n} dK_j^i) + \sum_{h=1}^{m^*} (\sum_{i=1}^{n} w_h \, dL_h^i)}{\sum_{i=1}^{m} r_j \, dK_j^1 + \sum_{h=1}^{m^*} w_h \, dL_h^1}$$

Now, when all factor prices are flexible and all factors are fully employed, we have

$$\sum_{i=1}^{n} dK_j^i = \sum_{i=1}^{n} dL_h^i = 0$$

for all $j = 1, 2, \ldots, m$ and $h = 1, 2, \ldots, m^*$.

Thus, the above equation can be simplified as

$$\frac{d(\sum_{i=2}^{n} p_i X_i)}{dX_1} = -p_1,$$

which implies that the slope of the transformation curve is equal to the relative commodity prices. For example when $n = 2$, the above equation reduces to $dX_2/dX_1 = -(p_1/p_2)$.

When factor-prices $w_1, w_2, \ldots, w_{m^*}$ are not flexible and factors

$L_1, \ldots, L_{m^*}$ are not fully employed, we generally have

$$\sum_{i=1}^{n} dL_h^i = dL_h \neq 0.$$

Thus,

$$\frac{d(\sum_{i=2}^{m} p_i X_i)}{dX_1} = -p_1 + \frac{\sum_{h=1}^{m^*} w_h \, dL_h}{\sum_{j=1}^{m} r_j \, dK_j^1 + \sum_{h=1}^{m^*} w_h \, dL_h^1}$$

is satisfied along the transformation curve.

Dixit [40] and Neary [71] showed that comparative statics analysis of this fix-factor-price economy can be easily conducted by using the following type of restricted revenue function:

$$R(p; K; w) = \{\max_X pX - wL \colon \text{s.t. } X = F(K; L)\},$$

where p is the commodity price vector, X the vector of output, K the vector of flexible-price factor endowments, L the vector of fix-price factor inputs, and w is the vector of given fixed factor prices of L-factors. It is easy to show that the partial derivatives of R with respect to p_i, K_j and w_h are

$$\partial R / \partial p_i = X_i,$$
$$\partial R / \partial K_j = r_j,$$
$$\partial R / \partial w_h = L_h.$$

See Neary [71] for the details of the analyses using this result.

2. SOME UNORTHODOX RESULTS IN MINIMUM-WAGE ECONOMIES

In minimum-wage economy models one can derive many results that do not hold in the standard trade models with flexible factor prices. As will become clear in the following discussion, these unorthodox results are due to the fact that the employment level changes with the relative commodity prices. It is a type of distortion. Minimum-wage economies thus carry various unorthodox results in the same way as other types of distorted economies do.[7] Although the relation that exists between the

---

[7] We do not discuss other types of distortions in this paper.

employment level and the relative commodity prices takes different
forms depending on the underlying model and the specification of
wage rigidity, we can make basically the same argument for all
cases. Therefore, most of the analysis in the present section is
restricted to the case of the specific-factors model discussed in
Section 1.1. Extensions to other cases are easy and therefore
omitted.

2.1. Gains from international trade

In a minimum-wage economy there is a possibility that autarky is
better than free trade. In order to see this, it is useful to review the
standard textbook exposition of gains from international trade for
an economy without distortions.

In Figure 9 the curve AB is the production frontier, and the
curves U_0, U_1 and U_2 are the indifference curves of the representative individual in the economy. The point E is an autarkic
equilibrium point and U_0 indicates the autarkic utility level. Suppose
that the economy starts trading the two goods with the rest of the

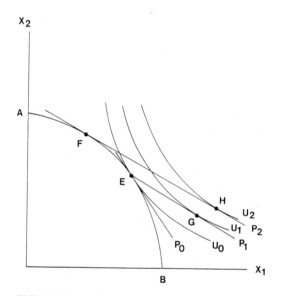

FIGURE 9   Production gains and consumption gains.

world under world prices of the two goods, say the prices indicated by the line p_2 in the figure. The point H then becomes the consumption point of the economy under free trade and U_2 is the utility level there. The production point is F.

Gains from international trade, which are indicated by the increase in utility from U_0 to U_2, can be divided into two types of gains: these are usually called consumption gains and production gains.

Consumption gains can be explained as follows. Suppose that there is no shift of the factors of production between the two sectors from the position of the autarkic equilibrium point E. Even in this case the budget line for the representative consumer shifts from the line p_0 to the line p_1, both of which are drawn in Figure 9. As a result of this shift of the budget line, the consumption point moves from E to G. Obviously the utility level is higher at the latter point. The economy can always enjoy consumption gains as long as the world prices under free trade are different from the economy's autarkic prices, since the marginal rate of substitution among commodities at the autarkic equilibrium point are different from the relative commodity prices under free trade.

Let us next explain production gains. The economy's autarkic price ratios are equal to the marginal rates of transformation among various commodities at the autarkic production point. As long as the relative prices under free trade are different from the economy's autarkic relative prices, it is possible to increase the economy's income level by expanding the output of the goods whose autarkic relative prices are lower than the relative prices under free trade and diminishing outputs of other goods. In Figure 9 the economy can increase its income level by moving to the north-west along the production frontier from its autarkic production point. The income level continues to rise until the production point reaches the point where the marginal rate of transformation is equal to the relative price under free trade. The point F illustrates this point. The rise in utility level due to this shift of production point is illustrated by the shift from the indifference curve U_1 to U_2.

A minimum-wage economy can enjoy consumption gains from international trade, but production gains from international trade for a minimum-wage economy may become negative. We can explain this by using Figure 10. ABC in the figure is the transforma-

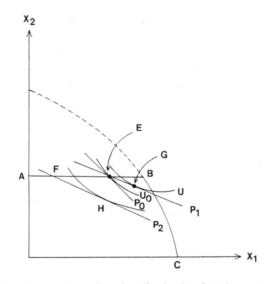

FIGURE 10 Consumption gain and production loss from international trade.

tion curve of the specific-factors economy with a minimum-wage restriction. The point E is the autarkic equilibrium point, U_0 is the utility level there, and the line p_0 indicates the autarkic price ratio.

Suppose that the line p_2 is the world relative price of the two goods under free trade. The point F becomes the production point of this economy under free trade and H is the corresponding consumption point. As shown in the figure, the utility level under free trade is lower than under autarky. This paradoxical result is due to the fact that the amount of employment in the economy decreases after the economy starts trading with the rest of the world: a fall in the relative price of good 1 decreases the amount of employment. Thus, the economy suffers a production loss from international trade rather than enjoying a production gain.

Note that the economy does enjoy consumption gains from international trade even in this case. If the production point of this economy stays at the point E, the consumption point will move from E to G, which indicates that there are consumption gains from international trade. The existence of consumption gains is easy to understand if we note that consumption gains are not related to the production activities of the economy, on which the minimum-wage has an impact.

Since the possibility of a loss from international trade is due to the change in the amount of employment caused by a price change, the economy may suffer from international trade under any type of wage rigidity as long as the amount of employment in the economy changes with the relative commodity prices.

2.2. The change in the terms of trade and industrial adjustment

The above discussion about the gains from international trade can be used to examine the welfare impact of a change in the terms of trade. The economy may suffer from an improvement of its terms of trade and may also suffer from a resource shift from declining sectors to other sectors. To illustrate these points in the simplest fashion, let us consider a small country with a two-good, specific-factors technology. As in Section 1.1, we consider the following production functions;

$$X_1 = F(L_1, K_1) = K_1 f(n_1)$$
$$X_2 = G(L_2, K_2) = K_2 g(n_2),$$

where

$$n_i = L_i / K_i \qquad i = 1, 2$$
$$f(n_1) = F(n_1, 1), \qquad g(n_2) = G(n_2, 1)$$

and all other notations are the same as those in Section 1.1. Labor is assumed to be mobile between the two sectors, but capital moves only gradually.

Suppose that the economy is originally located at the long-run equilibrium point, where there is no distortion. Thus, both labor and capital are fully employed, and factor prices are equalized between the two sectors. The point E in Figure 11 illustrates this original equilibrium production point. The curve AB in the figure is the long-run transformation curve of the economy when all factor prices are flexible and both factors can move freely between the two sectors. The line qq indicates the relative price of the two goods the economy is facing at the original equilibrium point. The point F is the consumption point. The economy is exporting good 2.

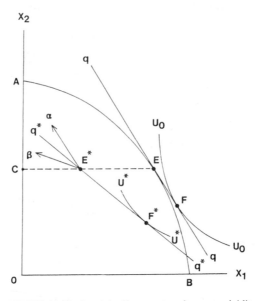

FIGURE 11   Industrial adjustment under wage rigidity.

Suppose now that the country's terms of trade (the relative price of good 2 in units of good 1) improves (say due to a price fall of good 1). If the production point does not change and stays at E, the utility level of the country will rise, since the country can now import a larger amount of good 1 in exchange for the same amount of exports of good 2. This utility gain from the appreciation of the terms of trade corresponds to the consumption gains from international trade discussed above.

If the factors can move freely between the two sectors so as to equalize the values of marginal productivities of the factors between the two sectors, the country can also enjoy production gains. A shift of factors of production from sector 1 to sector 2 raises the country's income level, and the country's utility level increases further. Note that income increases even if labor alone is mobile between the two sectors.

When the real wage is downward rigid, the story becomes quite different, and the country's utility level may fall as a result of an appreciation of the country's terms of trade. Haberler [10] is a classic paper that made this point.

Suppose that the real wage rate in units of good 2 is downward rigid and that capital does not move between the two sectors in the short-run. Then, as a result of a fall in the relative price of good 1 producers of good 1 faces a higher real wage. Thus, the employment level of sector 1 falls. (The employment level of sector 2 does not change.) As we explained in Section 1.1, the production point of the economy moves from E to the left along the line CE in Figure 11. (The curve CEB is the transformation curve under the wage rigidity assumed here.) The country's income level falls due to the shift of the production point. This phenomenon is exactly the same as the production loss from international trade that we discussed in the previous section.

Whether the overall impact of the appreciation of the terms of trade is positive or negative depends on the relative size of the consumption gain and the production loss. It is certainly possible that the country's utility level falls as a result of the appreciation of the terms of trade. Figure 11 illustrates this case. The point E^* in the figure is the production point after the change in the terms of trade. The line q^*q^* is the price line and the point F^* is the consumption point.

There is another unorthodox result in minimum-wage economies concerning industrial adjustment. At the new short-run equilibrium point E^* in Figure 11, the rental for capital is lower in sector 1 than in sector 2. Thus, capital will shift from the declining sector (sector 1) to other sector (sector 2). As discussed by Mussa [68] and Mayer [65], this type of resource shift is generally welfare-enhancing when factor prices are flexible. However, this is not necessarily the case in a minimum-wage economy. Neary [19] pointed out that the economy's utility level may fall as a result of the shift of resources. He called the phenomenon "immiserizing allocation". We can illustrate this in the present framework as follows.

At the short-run equilibrium E^*, the following conditions are satisfied:

$$w_0 = p^*f'(n_1^*) = g'(n_2^*)$$
$$r_1^* = p^*[f(n_1^*) - n_1^*f'(n_1^*)] < r_2^* = g(n_2^*) - n_2^*g'(n_2^*),$$

where p^* is the relative price of good 1 in units of good 2 at the short-run equilibrium, n_1^* and n_2^* are the labor-capital input ratios of the two sectors, w_0 is the downward rigid real wage rate measured in units of good 2, and r_1^* and r_2^* are the rentals for capital in the two sectors.

Due to the difference of r_1^* and r_2^*, capital starts moving slowly from sector 1 to 2. Let us assume that the real wage rate w_0 does not change. This assumption makes Neary's point simpler. In reality, w_0 will fall gradually in the process of industrial adjustment. But as long as the speed of the change in the wage rate is not high compared with the speed of the shift of capital between the industries, the basic result explained below holds.

If capital moves from sector 1 to sector 2 by the amount dK, the total employment and income level of the economy change in the following way:

$$dL = (n_2^* - n_1^*)\, dK$$
$$dY = p^*\, dX_1 + dX_2 = \{g(n_2^*) - p^* f(n_1^*)\}\, dK$$
$$= [(r_2^* - r_1^*) + w_0(n_2^* - n_1^*)]\, dK.$$

Of special interest is the case $n_1^* > n_2^*$: the case where the delining sector (sector 1) is more labor intensive than the other sector (sector 2) at the short-run equilibrium point E^*. In this case the shift of capital from sector 1 to 2 decreases the employment of the economy, since some labor thrown out of sector 1 as a result of the inter-industry capital movement is not hired in sector 2.

Furthermore, the income level may also fall. The condition for income to fall is

$$(r_2^* - r_1^*) + w_0(n_2^* - n_1^*) < 0.$$

The first term in the above condition, $(r_2^* - r_1^*)$, is positive. Therefore, this term works in the direction of increasing the income level. Since this term indicates the effect of capital reallocation between the two sectors on the income level, it is natural that the term is positive: the reallocation of capital from sector 1 to sector 2 is welfare-enhancing. The second term $w_0(n_2^* - n_1^*)$, on the other hand, is negative. This term indicates the negative effect of the decrease in employment on the income level. When the difference in the labor-capital ratio between the two sectors is large and when the minimum-wage level is high, this term becomes large.

There is a possibility that the second term dominates the first term. Two arrows from the point E^* (α and β) in Figure 11 illustrate possible directions of the shift of production as a result of the capital reallocation. The arrow α illustrates the case where capital reallocation is income increasing, while the arrow β illustrates the case where the above negative condition is satisfied.

2.3. Relaxing the wage constraint

Although the minimum-wage constraint is the source of all irregular behavior of the economy, relaxing the wage restriction does not necessarily enhance the welfare of the economy. Figure 12 illustrates the situation where the economy's utility level falls when the minimum-wage level is lowered.

When the minimum-wage level becomes lower, the transformation curve shifts outward from the position ABC to the position $A'B'C$ as shown in the figure. The points E and F depict the initial production and consumption point. The economy exports good 1.

The output of the two goods will expand in response to the fall in the minimum-wage level if the relative price of the two goods does

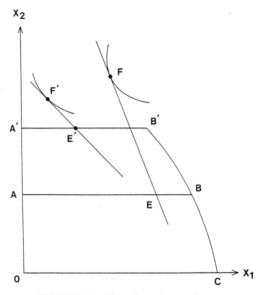

FIGURE 12   The effect of wage decrease.

not change. The situation considered here is essentially the same as the one dealt within the literature on immiserizing growth.[8] There are at least two cases where the economy's utility level falls as a result of outward expansion of the transformation curve: one is the case where the economy is large and the expansion of outputs worsens the country's terms of trade (Bhagwati [25]) and other is the case where the economy is small in the world market but imposes tariffs and/or subsidies and therefore faces a distortion (Johnson [54]).

As shown by Bhagwati [25], the negative welfare impact of deteriorating terms of trade may dominate the positive welfare impact of output expansion when the elasticity of import of the home country and that of the rest of the world are small. This property is satisfied in the present case as well. Furthermore, as we discussed before, the change in the terms of trade will affect the employment level. Thus, if the deterioration of the terms of trade lowers the employment level of the country, the country will suffer a further loss.

If the country is small in the world market, relaxing the minimum-wage constraint will generally raise the country's welfare level in the specific-factors model. This is so even if the country faces a distortion in the form of import tariffs. We cannot derive an example of Johnson-type immiserizing growth at least in the simple cases discussed in the previous section.

2.4. Transfer problem

Financial and commodity transfer from one country to other may have different welfare implication in a minimum-wage economy from those in an economy without distortions. In an economy without distortions the terms of trade does not change so much that the welfare impacts of the transfer are reversed. Thus, the transferor's utility level always fall and the recipient's utility level always rise. However, this is not true in a minimum-wage economy. This irregular result is not peculiar to a minimum-wage economy but is shared with other types of distorted economies. Although we

---

[8] See Bhagwati [25] and Johnson [54] for the problem of immiserizing growth.

restrict our discussion to the case of minimum-wage economies, extensions to other types of distortions are almost trivial.[9]

Consider a two-good, two-country model with goods 1 and 2 and the home and the foreign country. Assume that the foreign country makes a financial transfer to the home country. As a result of the transfer the terms of trade of the home country may change in either direction depending on the sizes of the two countries' marginal propensities to import. The home country's terms of trade will appreciate if and only if the sum of the two countries' marginal propensities is larger than one.[10] It is easy to see that this result is satisfied both in a flexible-price economy and in a minimum-wage economy, since the above argument is based only on the properties of demand behavior.

In flexible-price economies we can also prove the following property: the transferor (the foreign country here) always suffers and the recipient (the home country here) always gains from the transfer irrespective of the direction of the change in terms of trade.

It might be useful to show a rough proof of this property for a flexible-price economy.[11] The fact that the pre-transfer equilibrium is an efficient point in the sense of Pareto optimality of the world economy plays a crucial role in the proof.

In order to show the above property, suppose that the foreign country's (the transferor's) post-transfer terms of trade appreciates so much that its post-transfer utility level is just equal to its pre-transfer level.[12] Assume that the home country exports good 1 and the foreign country exports good 2. Since the post-transfer relative price of good 2 (the transferor's exportable good) is higher than the pre-transfer level, the foreign country's post-transfer export supply of good 2 is larger than the pre-transfer export level.

This can be easily confirmed by considering production and demand behavior separately. Only the substitution effect is working in production. Thus, an increase in the relative price of good 2

---

[9] Bhagwati, Brecher and Hatta [30], Brecher and Bhagwati [31] and Yano [90] deal with this issue.

[10] See Caves and Jones [33].

[11] The following proof is based on Caves and Jones [33].

[12] Our analysis is based on the existence of a utility function of the representative individual.

implies a larger production of good 2. To examine the change in demand behavior, we must consider both substitution and income effects. The substitution effect in demand works in the same direction as that in production. Since the terms of trade of the foreign country changes in such a way that the post-transfer utility level is equal to the pre-transfer level, the income effect is neutral. Thus, combining above effects through production and demand, we can conclude that the foreign country's export supply of good 2 is larger after the transfer than before the transfer.

The home country's post-transfer utility level cannot be higher than its pre-transfer level, for the following reason. Since the pre-transfer equilibrium point is efficient, the utility levels of the two countries cannot be raised together from that point. As the foreign country's post-transfer utility level is equal to its pre-transfer level, the home country's post-transfer utility level cannot be higher than the pre-transfer level. It is now easy to see that as long as good 2 is normal, the home country's import demand for good 2 is smaller after the transfer than before the transfer. Substitution effects and the income effect work in the same direction.

We thus have shown that good 2 will be in excess supply in the world market under the relative price under which the foreign country's post-transfer utility level is equal to its pre-transfer level. Therefore, if the Marshall–Lerner stability condition is satisfied, the post-transfer relative price of good 2 should be lower than the level assumed above. This implies that the foreign country's post-transfer utility level is lower than the pre-transfer utility level.[13] Note also that a similar argument can be used to show that there is no possibility that the recipient's post-transfer utility level is lower than the pre-transfer level.

Let us now examine how the above argument changes in a minimum-wage economy. Minimum-wage economies do not carry the property that the pre-transfer trade equilibrium is Pareto efficient. Due to the lack of the Pareto-efficiency property it is easy to construct examples under which either the transferor gains from the transfer or the recipient suffers a loss, or both occur. We explain only the case where both the transferor and the recipient gain from

---

[13] We implicitly assume the uniqueness of the post-transfer equilibrium.

the transfer. Other types of unorthodox results can be obtained in a similar manner.

Consider a two-good, two-country specific-factors trade model, in which the foreign country exports good 2 and makes a transfer to the home country. Suppose that the real wage rate in units of good 1 (the home country's exportable good) is downward rigid both in the home and in the foreign country. Now, if the sum of the two country's marginal propensities to import is larger than one, the transfer from the foreign to the home country will raise the relative price of good 2 (an appreciation of the foreign country's terms of trade).

Suppose that the relative price of good 2 rises so much that the foreign country's post-transfer utility level is just equal to its pre-transfer level. If we can show that good 2 is in excess demand at this price ratio, then the stability condition can be used to show that the post-transfer equilibrium price ratio is higher and that the foreign country (the transferor) gains from the transfer. The key to our argument lies in the change in production and consumption of the home country. Since the home country is a minimum-wage economy in the sense assumed above, the increase in the relative price of good 2 will expand the volume of employment there. As we have already shown, the positive welfare impact of the expansion of the volume of employment may dominate the negative welfare impact of the deterioration of the terms of trade. Suppose that this is the case. Then it is possible that the home country's net import demand for good 2 increases. This arises when consumption and production elasticities of substitution between the two goods are small relative to the effect through the expansion of employment. Thus, the world demand for good 2 might exceed the world supply of the same good at the relative price under which the post-transfer transferor's utility level is equal to its pre-transfer level. In this case both countries gain from the transfer.

2.5. Foreign investment in minimum-wage economies

Das [37] analyzes the impact of capital inflow on a minimum-wage economy. His model differs from the ones discussed above in one respect: there is a non-traded good. When a non-traded good is introduced, we have another route for irregular results. Since the relative price of non-traded goods and traded goods is determined endogenously even in a small country, any exogeneous change such as capital inflow and devaluation, which affect the relative price, will change the volume of employment.[14]

In a minimum-wage economy in which some labor is unemployed, capital inflow may increase the volume of unemployment through the change in the relative price of non-traded and traded goods. Das showed this result.

To see the above result, consider a small-country, two-good trade model where good 1 is a tradable good and good 2 is a non-tradable good. The production structure of the two sectors is given by the specific-factors technology discussed in Section 1.1. Furthermore, the real wage rate in units of good 1 is assumed to be downward rigid.

As in Section 1.1, the outputs of the two goods can be expressed as

$$X_1 = K_1 f(n_1) \tag{2.1}$$

$$X_1 = K_2 g(n_2), \tag{2.2}$$

where notations are the same as those in Section 2.2. Note that the labor-capital input ratios n_1 and n_2 are given by the following marginal conditions:

$$f'(n_1) = w, \qquad pg'(n_2) = w, \tag{2.3}$$

where w is the minimum-wage rate of this economy, and p is the relative price of good 2 in units of good 1. The relative price p is determined by the equilibrium condition in the non-tradable good (good 2) market:

$$D(p, I) = X_2 \tag{2.4}$$

where $D(p, I)$ is the demand function for good 2 (non-tradable good) and I is the real income measured in units of good 1, which can be expressed as

$$I = w(L_1 + L_2) + r_1 K_1 + r_2 K_2, \tag{2.5}$$

---

[14] The introduction of a non-traded good has another important implication: with a non-traded good, the Keynesian unemployment situation, which will be discussed in Sections 4 through 7, becomes relevant even for a small open economy.

where r_1 and r_2 are the rentals for capital in the two sectors both measured in units of good 1. We assume that the minimum-wage rate w is so high that some labor is unemployed.

Let us now examine the impact of the capital inflow into the non-tradable good (good 2) sector on the relative price and the employment level. Suppose that dJ units of capital flows into the second industry. For simplicity it is assumed that originally there is no foreign capital used in the production of good 2 in the domestic economy. This capital inflow causes the following output change in sector 2:

$$dX_2 = g(n_1)\, dJ + K_2 g'(n_2)\, dn_2, \qquad (2.6)$$

where dn_2, the change in the labor-capital input ratio, is given by

$$dn_2/dp = -(g'/g'')/p \qquad (2.7)$$

Differentiating the equation for the income level I, we obtain

$$dI = w\, dL_2 + K_2\, dr_2 = wK_2\, dn_2 + n_2\, dJ + gK_2\, dp \qquad (2.8)$$

Substituting (2.6) and (2.7) and (2.8) into

$$D_p\, dp + D_I\, dI = dX_2, \qquad (2.9)$$

we obtain

$$dp/dJ = [-D_I wn_2 + g(n_2)]/H,$$

where

$$H = D_p + D_I g(\ ')K_2 + (D_I - 1/p)[wK_2(-g'/g'')/p] < 0$$

and the negative sign of H is the stability condition for the non-tradable good (good 2) market.

Thus, the price of the non-tradable good falls as a result of capital-inflow if and only if

$$g(n_2) - D_I wn_2 > 0$$

This result is easy to interpret. If the relative price of the two goods stays at the initial level, a capital inflow into the second industry of dJ will increase the supply of good 2 by the amount $g(n_2)$ and increase the demand for good 2 through an increase in I by the amount $D_I wn_2$. If the stability condition is satisfied, the direction of the change in p is determined by the relative size of these two terms.

Let us next examine the impact of a capital inflow on the country's employment level. Since the employment in sector 1 does not change, we need to examine only the change in the employment in sector 2, which can be expressed as:

$$dL_1 = K_2\,dn_2 + n_2\,dJ$$
$$= [n_2 + K_2(dn_2/dp)(dp/dJ)]\,dJ$$
$$= [n_2 + K_2(-g'/g'')(1/p)\{g(n_2) - D_I wn_2\}/H]\,dJ$$

Thus, $dL_2/dJ < 0$ if and only if

$$D_p + D_I g K_2 + K_2(-g'/g'')(g - n_2 g')[1/(pn_2)] > 0$$

This result can be interpreted as follows. Suppose that the price p falls in such a way that the employment level of sector 2 stays at the same level as before the capital inflow. Then the supply of and demand for the non-tradable good will change in the following way:

$$dX_2 = [g(n_2) - n_2 g'(n_2)]\,dJ$$
$$dD = D_I\,dI + D_p\,dp = [D_I(dr_2/dp)K_2 + D_p](dp/dJ)\,dJ$$

Note that the change in the supply dX_2 is positive, while the change in the demand dD can be either positive or negative: the first term in dD, that is, $D_I\,dI$ is negative, while the second term $D_p\,dp$ is positive.

There will be an excess supply in the market of non-tradable good at the price considered here if and only if

$$dX_2 - dD = [(g - n_2 g')\,dJ - D_I(dr_2/dp)K_2(dp_2/dJ)]\,dJ$$
$$- D_p(dp/dJ)\,dJ > 0$$

If the above inequality is satisfied, the stability condition can be used to prove that the equilibrium price level p falls so far that the amount of employment decreases as a result of capital inflow into the non-tradable good sector.

It is easy to see that the employment level of the economy falls as a result of a capital inflow when the demand for the non-tradable good is not price elastic. In this case, an expansion of the output of the non-tradable good due to capital inflow will reduce the price of the non-tradable good significantly, as a result of which the employment level in the non-tradable good sector is reduced.

3. COMMERCIAL POLICIES IN MINIMUM-WAGE ECONOMIES

The economic implications of commercial policies in a minimum-wage economy are quite different from those in an economy without distortions. The difference comes from the fact that wage rigidity imposes a distortion in production in such a way that the slope of the transformation curve is not equal to the relative commodity price. Thus, the problem of commercial policies in a minimum-wage economy is a special case of a more general problem, namely commercial policies in distorted economies.

Distortions caused by a minimum-wage constraint have the following implications for the effects of commercial policies.

(1) The imposition of a protection policy by one country may enhance the utility levels of all countries, since free trade equilibrium is not Pareto efficient from the world welfare view point when some country is subject to a minimum-wage distortion. This contrasts with the case of an undistorted economy, where commercial policy by any country always hurts some other country (this may be the country imposing the policy).[15]

(2) Since wage rigidity is the origin of the distortion, the first best policy from the national welfare view point must involve the removal of wage-rigidity. A subsidy on wage payment can be used to remove the distortion.

(3) When wage subsidies cannot be used, the choice of commercial policy becomes the problem of second best policy. It is not generally possible to achieve full employment without removing the minimum-wage restriction. This second best policy has the following two features: (i) It is always desirable to introduce production taxes or subsidies, since the marginal rate of transformation in production is not equal to relative commodity prices, and (ii) when production taxes and subsidies cannot be used and taxes and subsidies on trade are the only available policy instruments, then the desirable form of

---

[15] Hillman [49] discusses this case.

trade taxes and subsidies can take various forms depending on the underlying structure of trade and distortion.

(4) The welfare ranking of various policies for achieving such objectives as restriction of consumption and restriction of imports may not be the same as in an undistorted economy. For example, an import tax may not be the best policy to restrict the import of some goods.

3.1. The first best policy

Since a downward rigid wage is the source of trouble in a minimum-wage economy, the first best policy is the one that relieves the economy from the minimum-wage constraint. Subsidies on wage payments financed by a lump-sum tax can be used for this purpose. The economy can achieve full employment of labor by a wage subsidy.

For a small open economy, whose terms of trade is given by the economic conditions of the rest of the world, a wage subsidy alone is enough to achieve the first best point. This is true for all types of wage rigidity discussed in the first section. As long as the amount of a wage subsidy is large enough for labor to be fully employed, production will take place at the point on the production frontier at which the slope of the frontier is equal to the world relative price.

For a large open economy, the first best policy must involve an optimal import tax (or an export tax), since the country has monopoly power in the world market. Thus, both wage subsidies and import taxes are necessary to maximize the country's welfare.

The point E in Figure 13 illustrates the first best consumption point of a large open economy. The curve HCB in the figure is the transformation curve of this minimum-wage economy. The figure pictures a specific-factors model with the wage rate in units of good 2 downward rigid. The curve AFB is the production frontier of the economy, namely the set of production points that the economy can achieve by using given factor endowments in an efficient way. A wage subsidy is necessary in order to reach this production frontier.

The curve KFJ is the so-called Baldwin consumption possibility frontier of this economy.[16] The consumption possibility frontier can

---

[16] See Baldwin [21] for the consumption frontier.

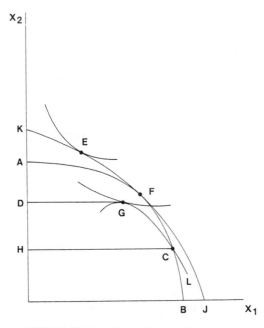

FIGURE 13   First best and second best points.

be drawn by sliding the origin of the foreign offer curve, GCL in the figure, along the production possibility frontier. The Baldwin consumption possibility frontier is the set of the consumption points that the economy can attain through production and international trade. The first best point is depicted by the point on the Baldwin consumption possibility frontier at which the indifference curve is tangential to the frontier.

3.2. The second best policy

When wage subsidies cannot be used, some labor remains unemployed and the production point is restricted to the rigid-wage transformation curve (HCB in Figure 13). Thus, the second best policy is the one that attains the best point on this rigid-wage transformation curve.

Note that we can draw a consumption possibility frontier corresponding to this rigid-wage transformation curve just as we drew the Baldwin consumption possibility frontier in the previous sub-section. The curve $DGCB$ in Figure 13 illustrates a rigid-wage consumption possibility frontier, which can be drawn by sliding the origin of the foreign offer curve along the rigid-wage transformation curve. The second best point is then given by the point at which an indifference curve is tangential to this consumption frontier.

To achieve this second best point, it is necessary to use not only trade taxes (or subsidies) but also production or consumption taxes (or subsidies). The following marginal condition must be satisfied at the second best point:[17]

$$DRT = FRT = DRS \qquad (3.1)$$

where DRT is the marginal domestic rate of transformation in production between the two goods (the slope of the transformation curve), FRT is the marginal foreign rate of trade (i.e., the slope of the foreign offer curve), and DRS is the marginal domestic rate of transformation in consumption (i.e. the slope of the indifference curve). Since the transformation curve might have a kinked point, the above condition should be modified for that case. We do not mention this point in the following, since the modification is trivial.

In a flexible price economy, DRT and DRS are equalized by the market mechanism. However, in a minimum-wage economy DRT and DRS are not generally equal. The government must introduce production taxes (subsidies) or consumption taxes (subsidies) in order to equalize these two marginal rates of transformation. Since DRT can be larger or smaller than DRS at the free trade equilibrium point depending on the underlying wage rigidity, the form of the second best production (or consumption) taxes (subsidies) cannot be determined without specifying details of the model.

As for the form of trade taxes (subsidies) in the second best policy, we can make the same argument as we did in the first best policy. For a small open economy FRT is equal to the world relative commodity price. Since this relative price is equal to DRS under free trade, the government need not introduce any trade taxes. What is necessary to achieve the second best point is to introduce a production tax (or subsidy) to make DRT equal to DRS.

---

[17] See Bhagwati [27] for this marginal condition.

For a large open economy the optimal tariff argument can be applied. *FRT* is no longer equal to the world relative commodity price. If good 2 is the economy's import good in a two-good trade model, *FRT* and the world relative price p_1/p_2 are related in the following way:

$$FRT = (p_1/p_2)[1 - (1/\varepsilon^*)],$$

where ε^* is the elasticity of the foreign import of good 1 with respect to the foreign terms of trade (p_2/p_1).[18]

It is now obvious that both trade taxes and production taxes must be introduced in order to have the marginal condition (3.1) for the second best point. The point *G* in Figure 13 illustrates the second best consumption point and the point *C* is the corresponding production point. To achieve the production point *C* it is necessary to introduce a production tax on good 2 (or a production subsidy on good 1). To achieve the consumption (trade) point *G*, at which *FRT* is equal to the slope of the line p_1 and the world relative price is equal to the slope of the line p_2, the government must introduce an import tariff.

3.3. The case where only trade taxes and subsidies can be used

Let us next consider the case where the government can use only taxes and subsidies on imports and exports. The economy then cannot achieve the second best point that we have discussed above, since the three marginal values *DRT*, *FRT*, and *DRS* cannot be equalized by trade policies alone.

In order to analyze the third best trade policies, it is useful to use the following equation indicating the change in the utility level of the economy:[19]

$$dy = dc_1 + p\, dc_2 = (dx_1 + p\, dx_2) + (p - p^*)\, dM - M\, dp^*, \quad (3.2)$$

where p is the domestic relative price of good 2 in terms of good 1, p^* is the relative price of good 2 in the rest of the world, c_i $(i = 1, 2)$

---

[18] We assume that the foreign country is engaged in free trade. See, for example, Caves and Jones [33] for the derivation of this condition. See also Section 3.3.

[19] This equation can be derived by differentiating the utility function and by substituting trade balance condition into the differential form of the utility function. See Caves and Jones [33] for the derivation.

is the consumption of good i, x_i is the production of good i, and M is the amount of import of good 2, namely,

$$M = c_2 - x_2.$$

It is assumed that the economy imports good 2.

This equation can be interpreted as follows. The term $dc_1 + p\,dc_2$ indicates the change in the utility level of the country measured in units of good 1. The first term in the right hand side of (3.2) represents the change in the value (in terms of good 1) of the domestic output, where the domestic relative price p is used for the valuation. The second term $(p - p^*)\,dM$ is the contribution of the change of imports to domestic welfare: if imports of good 2 are restricted by a tariff and $p - p^* = tp^* > 0$ is satisfied, where t is an ad valoren tariff rate, then an increase in M contributes to an increase in domestic welfare.

The third term in the right hand side of (3.2) indicates the effect of a change in the home country's terms of trade $(1/p^*)$ on domestic welfare. The amount of the change in utility due to an appreciation of the terms of trade is proportional to the amount of import M. This is nothing but the income effect in the Slutzky equation.

Before discussing the nature of the third best trade policies in a minimum-wage economy, it will be useful to briefly summarize the results on trade policies in a flexible price economy. In a flexible price economy, where the slope of the transformation curve (DRT) is equal to the domestic relative price $(1/p)$,

$$dx_1 + p\,dx_2 = 0$$

is satisfied in (3.2) as long as the change in question is along the transformation curve. Since our concern here is the impact of a change in trade policies on the resource allocation of the economy, this condition is satisfied. Thus, (3.2) can be simplified as

$$dy = (p - p^*)\,dM - M\,dp^* \qquad (3.3)$$

Using (3.3) the following well known results can be derived: (1) for a small open economy free trade is the best policy; (2) a large open economy can increase its utility level by restricting its imports, and the optimal import tariff rate in the case of a two-good trade model is equal to $1/(\varepsilon^* - 1)$, where ε^* is the elasticity of foreign import with respect to the relative price of the two goods.

Although these are well known results, it is useful for later use to present brief proofs of the results.

For a small open economy, the terms of trade $(1/p^*)$ is given exogenously, and therefore $dp^* = 0$ is satisfied. Thus, the first order condition $dy = 0$ is satisfied at the point where

$$p = p^*$$

holds. The free trade equilibrium point satisfies the above condition. It is easy to show that the free trade point also satisfies the second order condition for utility maximization.

For a large open economy, dp^* is not equal to zero and therefore the free trade equilibrium point is not optimal for the economy. Since imposition of an infinitesimal import tariff at the free trade point generally improves the terms of trade of the country, dp^* becomes negative for the policy. Thus, at the free trade point, $dy = -M \, dp^*$ becomes positive for an infinitesimal import tariff. By restricting its imports in an appropriate way, a large open economy can increase its welfare.

The optimal tariff rate can be derived from the first order condition:

$$dy = (p - p^*) \, dM - M \, dp^* = tp^* \, dM - M \, dp^* = 0 \qquad (3.4)$$

where t is an *ad valorem* tariff rate. (It is easy to check that the second order condition is satisfied at the optimal point.) The optimal tariff rate t can be written as

$$t = \hat{p}^*/\hat{M}, \qquad (3.5)$$

where the hat notation "^" indicates the rate of change of the variable, say $\hat{x} = dx/x$. By differentiating the trade equilibrium condition

$$p^*M = M^*, \qquad (3.6)$$

where M^* is the foreign import of good 1, we obtain

$$\hat{p}^* + \hat{M} = \hat{M}^* = \varepsilon^*\hat{p}^*, \qquad (3.7)$$

where

$$\varepsilon^* = \hat{M}^*/\hat{p}^* \qquad (3.8)$$

is the foreign elasticity of import. By substituting (3.7) and (3.8) into (3.5), we obtain

$$t = 1/(\varepsilon^* - 1). \qquad (3.9)$$

Let us next consider a minimum-wage economy and compare it with the flexible price economy. In a minimum-wage economy the term $dx_1 + p\, dx_2$ does not vanish, since the slope of the transformation curve is not generally equal to the relative domestic price. Due to this property, we obtain the following result: "free trade is not the best trade policy for a small open economy".

The proof of this result is immediate. As we have seen above, the second and third terms in (3.2) become zero at the free trade point for a small open economy. Therefore,

$$dy = dx_1 + p\, dx_2 \neq 0,$$

is satisfied at the free trade point. Thus, trade intervention which increases the value of the domestic output (evaluated by the domestic prices) will improve the country's welfare. The welfare-enhancing trade intervention may be import taxes (export taxes) or import subsidies (export subsidies), depending on the underlying pattern of distortion. It is important to realize that not only the country imposing the welfare-enhancing trade interventions but also its trade partners may gain from the policy. This is because of the fact that the free trade equilibrium point is not Pareto efficient in a minimum-wage economy.

For a large open economy, we can prove the following result: "an import subsidy or free trade can be an optimal policy for a large country". For a large open economy the optimal tariff rate can be detived from the first order condition

$$dy = (dx_1 + p\, dx_2) + tp^*\, dM - M\, dp^* = 0. \qquad (3.10)$$

Thus, the optimal tariff rate t is

$$\begin{aligned}
t &= \hat{p}^*/\hat{M} - (dx_1 + p\, dx_2)/(p^*\, dM) \\
&= 1/(1 - \varepsilon^*) - (dx_1 + p\, dx_2)/(p\, dM^*). \qquad (3.11)
\end{aligned}$$

It is easy to see that the optimal tariff rate can be zero or negative if the second term of (3.11) is negative and dominates the first term: in other words, the optimal tariff rate becomes non-positive when the employment expansion effect of import subsidies (export subsidies) dominates the monopolistic effect of the tariff.

3.4. Noneconomic objectives

Within the standard two-commodity, two-factor model, Bhagwati and Srinivasan [26] examine the changes in the marginal conditions of optimal resource allocation brought about by the addition of a further constraint, a so-called noneconomic objective.[20] Different noneconomic objectives can be considered for an open economy. In the simple trade-theoretic model, where there are two final traded goods, we may distinguish three types of noneconomic objectives:

1) the production of a good should not fall below a certain level,

2) the consumption of a good should not exceed a certain level, and

3) the import (export) of a good should not exceed a certain level.

The optimal policy for achieving these noneconomic objectives can be characterized in the following way: the optimal policy is to intervene directly in the particular market to which the non-economic objective is addressed. Thus, production subsidies (taxes) are the optimal policy for the first objective above, consumption taxes (subsidies) are the optimal one for the second objective, and trade taxes (subsidies) are the optimal for the third objective.

These results on the optimal policy for noneconomic objectives do not hold in minimum-wage economies because of the existence of distortions in production.

It is useful for our purpose to present a brief proof of the Bhagwati–Srinivasan result for a flexible price economy to understand the basic nature of the problem and to see the reason why the result does not hold in a minimum-wage economy. We restrict our discussion to the case of the third objective, namely the case where the amount of import is restricted below a certain level.

Consider a one-consumer, two-good, small open economy. The production possibility frontier of this economy is denoted by the function $F(X_1, X_2)$ so that the pair of X_1 and X_2 satisfying the equation

$$F(X_1, X_2) = 0$$

---

[20] See Bhagwati [29] on this problem.

is the output levels of the two goods on the production frontier. (X_i is the output of good i, $i = 1, 2$.) The utility of the representative consumer is given by the utility function

$$U(c_1, c_2),$$

where c_i ($i = 1, 2$) is the consumption of good i. Both the utility function and the production function are assumed to have normal shapes.

The optimal policy for a noneconomic objective can be written by the following constrained maximization problem:

$$\max_{c_i, X_i} U(c_1, c_2)$$

subject to

$$F(X_1, X_2) = 0, \tag{3.12}$$

$$p_1 c_1 + p_2 c_2 = p_1 X_1 + p_2 X_2 \tag{3.13}$$

$$c_2 - X_2 \leqq \bar{M}, \tag{3.14}$$

where p_i ($i = 1, 2$) is the world price of good i, *which* is exogenously given due to the assumption of a small country, and $\bar{M}$ is the target ceiling of the import level of good 2. We assume that the amount of import of good 2 under free trade is larger than the level $\bar{M}$. (Thus, good 1 is an exportable good and good 2 is an importable good.)

If there is an interior solution to the above problem, the solution must satisfy the following first order condition:

$$U_2/U_1 = F_2/F_1 = p_2/p_1 + k,$$

where k is a positive number. This condition can be read as follows: the marginal rate of substitution in consumption (U_2/U_1), which is equal to the relative consumer price of the two goods, is equal to the marginal rate of transformation (F_2/F_1), which is equal to the relative producer price, and both are higher than the world relative price of the two goods p_2/p_1 by the amount k. The amount of difference k depends on the level of $\bar{M}$. It is obvious that the policy that can be used to achieve this condition is an import tariff on good 2 by the amount k (measured in terms of good 1). The combination of a production subsidy on good 2 and a consumption tax on good 2, both by the amount k in terms of good 1, has the same effect.

It is now easy to see that the above results do not hold in a minimum-wage economy, since F_2/F_1, the slope of the transformation curve is not equal to the relative producer price of the two goods. Figure 14 illustrates a case where import tariffs are not the optimal policy for the objective of restricting import.

This figure is based on the specific-factors model with a minimum-wage constraint in terms of good 2, whose properties we discussed in Section 1.1. The kinked curve BEF is the transformation curve of this economy. The terms of trade of this economy (the relative price of the two goods in the rest of the world) is depicted by the line p. The production point of this economy under free trade is G and the consumption point is H. Thus, this country will import good 2 by the amount of M under free trade.

Suppose that the government restricts the imports of good 2 below or equal to the level $\bar{M}$ (depicted on the vertical axis of the figure). We assume that the minimum-wage constraint is binding in the sense that the government cannot use the first best wage subsidy policy. Thus, the production point is restricted to the transformation curve BEF.

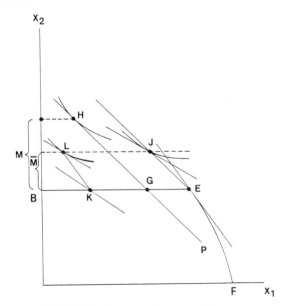

FIGURE 14   Optimal policy to restrict imports.

The optimal production point and consumption under this non-economic objective are given respectively by the points E and J in the figure. In this case, a production tax on good 2 and a consumption tax on good 2 is the optimal policy. (The tax rate and the subsidy rate are not generally the same.) The production and consumption points achieved by an import tariff are illustrated by the points K and L.

4. EARLY MACRO DISEQUILIBRIUM THEORIES

4.1. Early Keynesian models

The first postulate of the classical economics was assumed in Keynes's *General Theory* [58]. Apart from the fact that the counter-cyclical changes in real wages, which were derived from the postulate, were not confirmed empirically, with this assumption the Keynesian revolution is not through-going theoretically, since it implies that competitive firms are able to sell all of their output resulting from the prevailing market price. In other words, firms are not constrained in the product market by insufficient effective demand which makes involuntary unemployment, i.e., excess supply appear in the labor market. It is natural that recent quantity constraint disequilibrium theories do not regard unemployment in such a case as typically Keynesian and consider it as a boundary between classical and Keynesian unemployment.

In the field of international trade theory, Meade [16]–Tsiang [87] models have the same difficulty. They also assume the first postulate (the money wage rate paid in each employment is equal to the money value of the marginal physical product of labour in that employment, Meade [16, p. 11]) and rigid money wages (we constitute our standard policy combination by assuming that money wage-rates are fixed, Meade [16, p. 11]). Since the levels of output of internationally traded goods are fully determined by the given prices of output and wages in the case of a small country, furthermore, an increase in effective demand has no effect on the level of employment in the face of unemployment and merely results in larger deficits in the balance of payments, unless non-traded goods exist. As we shall see, however, this difficulty remains even in some recent models in the disequilibrium theory of international trade.

Consider next the case of Harberger [12]–Kemp [57, pp. 273–276] models of Keynesian underemployment economies with price rigidities. Let us denote the level of output, the demand for home goods, the demand for imports and the desired and existing amounts of monetary stock for country 1 by X, D, M, A and $\bar{A}$, respectively, and those of country 2 by the same notation with an asterisk. The equilibrium condition for the commodity markets is

$$X = D(X, R, A(X, R) - \bar{A}, A(X, R))$$
$$+ M^*(X^*, R, A^*(X^*, R) - \bar{A}^*, A^*(X^*, R)) \quad (4.1)$$

$$X^* = D^*(X^*, R, A^*(X^*, R) - \bar{A}^*, A^*(X^*, R))$$
$$+ M(X, R, A(X, R) - \bar{A}, A(X, R)) \quad (4.2)$$

where the rate of exchange R (the price of the currency of the country 2 in terms of that of the country 1) stands also for the relative price of home and foreign goods and X, D, M^*, A and $\bar{A}$ are in terms of the currency of country 1 and X^*, D^*, M, A^* and $\bar{A}^*$ are in terms of the currency of the country 2. The equilibrium condition for the money market is

$$A - \bar{A} = 0 \quad (4.3)$$

$$A^* - \bar{A}^* = 0, \quad (4.4)$$

where one of equations (4.1)–(4.4) is redundant because of Walras' law. In the case of floating exchange rates, X, X^* and R are determined from any three of (4.1)–(4.4), given $\bar{A}$ and $\bar{A}^*$. On the other hand, in the case of fixed exchange rates, (4.1) and (4.2) determine X and X^* given R, and $A - \bar{A}(A^* - \bar{A}^*)$ gives the balance of trade in terms of the currency of the country 1 (2).

In Harberger–Kemp models, the first postulate is not assumed. Each country is, however, assumed to be completely specialized to the production of the goods that she is exporting and real wages are assumed to be constant only in terms of such goods. The latter is unsatisfactory for some advanced countries importing considerable wage goods where the cost of living is highly dependent on the price of imported goods. It may be said that real wages are assumed to be constant from the domestic producers' point of view but not from the point of view of the worker-consumers. This difficulty can, however, be cleared though the model becomes complicated. The assumption of complete specialization is necessary since, without the first postulate, there is no rule for distributing domestic demand between foreign exporting producers and domestic import competing producers, if countries are incompletely specialized. In other words, it is due to the nonexistence of a Keynesian microeconomic foundation for macroeconomics to replace the discarded classical microfoundation, i.e., the first postulate. Surely it is unsatisfactory to assume away the existence of import competing industries. We must admit, however, that this problem has not yet been fully solved even in recent disequilibrium theories of international trade.

4.2. Early models of repressed inflation

Michaely [17] discussed the domestic effects of devaluation under repressed inflation which was "the rule rather than exception in most European countries during the war and early postwar period." The market is divided into a controlled and a noncontrolled sector and prices remain fixed in spite of excess demands in the former while excess demand or supply is cleared by changes in prices in the latter. Michaely regards this division inevitable since, otherwise, i.e., if all prices are subjected to control, the supply of labor will decline to the point at which incomes are just sufficient to buy the available controlled commodities, which implies further cuts in production, shortages even more severe than before, a further deline in the labor supply, and so on. Import prices are controlled and the supply of foreign exchange is assumed to be constant, so that the quantity of imports is constant. Production in each sector is also given, since complete immobility of resources between sectors as well as initial full employment are assumed.

When devaluation is taken in conjunction with domestic stabilization measures to prevent further increases of demand, an increase results in expenditures on imports in domestic currency since the quantity of imports is assumed to be unchanged. Because the amount of money is fixed, and imports belong exclusively to the controlled sector, devaluation represents an increase in expenditure in the controlled sector and a reduction in outlays in the noncontrolled sector. On the other hand, devaluation will raise the foreign demand curve for exports vertically, because constant demand prices in terms of foreign currency imply prices in domestic currency increased by devaluation. Since the quantity demanded must be equal to the constant quantity supplied in the free sector, Michaely considered the change in the domestic price level in the free sector that will just offset these effects of devaluation on the quantity demanded, domestically as well as from abroad, in the sector.

For this purpose, it is necessary to know the elasticity of domestic demand for goods and services in the noncontrolled sector. Michaely argued that this elasticity can be higher than it would have been had the commodities of the controlled sector also been free. He skillfully considered in Figure 15 the case of an individual consumer who is constrained by the existence of excess demand in the controlled market. W is a comoodity representative of the free sector, while V is a representative controlled commodity. With the budget line cc, the individual would be in equilibrium at C', were the markets entirely free. The quantity of V is, however, rationed at the level of $0K$. He will now be at the point C instead of C' in his "restrained equilibrium." If the price of W rises, so that the budget line becomes bb, the consumer will move to point B, whereas in a universally free market he would have moved to B'.

The movement from C to B represents a larger reduction in the quantity of W demanded than the movement from C' to B'. This is

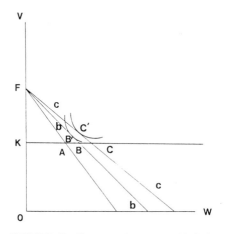

FIGURE 15   Consumer in repressed inflation.

because not only the substitution effect but also the entire weight of the income effect operates to reduce the quantity of W demanded. The elasticity of demand for W, the noncontrolled commodity, is thus higher in the constrained equilibrium than in the nonconstrained one.

Michaely paid due attention, carefully, to such disequilibrium phenomena as, for example, the effects on consumption of past accumulations of forced savings or excess liquidity. Although he emphasized the cumulative decline in the labor supply in the case in which all prices are controlled, however, he does not seem to regard the same problem as serious in the case where there exists a noncontrolled sector. Since the products of controlled and noncontrolled sectors are not perfectly substitutable, the possibility of a cumulative decline in labor supply may not be denied in the latter case if it exists in the former. Though smaller than in the case where all prices are perfectly flexible and there are no excess demands, however, a constant, unchanged supply of labor can be expected even in the case where all prices are controlled and excess demand prevails everywhere, as the recent disequilibrium theories will expain by the use of quantity constraint models.

The same problem was also considered by Kemp [13] under different assumptions. The prices of home-produced goods are assumed to be inflexible and an excess of demand over supply exists in the market for home-produced goods. As in the Keynesian case, the import-competing industries are assumed away and "the excess demand for home-produced goods spills into the market for imported goods," which is cleared by changes in the price in terms of foreign currency. Employment is assumed "not only full but constant" so that total home output is constant at the full employment level. Since the entire output is sold at a price which is pegged in terms of home currency, "aggregate money income is invariant under changes in the rate of exchange," if foreigners are free to buy unlimited quantities at the going price and domestic buyers receive the residue in the face of excess demand for home-produced goods.

The model of this export priority case is as follows.

$$M_1^d(Rp, E_1) - M_1^s(p) = 0 \qquad (4.5)$$

where M_1^d is the home import demand function, M_1^s is the foreign export supply function, R is the price of foreign currency in terms of home currency, p is the price of home imports in terms of foreign currency and E_1 is the excess demand for home products.

$$E_1 - H_1(pR) - M_2^d(1/R) = -C \qquad (4.6)$$

where H_1 is the home demand function for home-produced goods, M_2^d is the foreign import demand function and C is the home full employment output.

$$Z - (1/R)M_2^d(1/R) + pM_1^d(Rp, E_1) = 0 \qquad (4.7)$$

where Z is the home balance of payments in foreign currency.

From (4.5), (4.6) and (4.7) we can determine p, E_1 and Z when C and R are given, and know the changes in p, E_1 and Z induced by a change in R.

If home output is allocated, independently of the values assumed by other economic variables, between foreign and domestic buyers, foreign buyers pay the demand price for the quantity allocated to them. Therefore the value of home exports is constant in terms of foreign currency. Then in terms of home currency, the value of exports is proportional to the rate of exchange. Home money income now changes when the rate of exchange changes.

The model in the case of output allocation is as follows.

$$M_1^d(Rp, Y_1, E_1) - M_1^s(p) = 0 \qquad (4.8)$$

$$E_1 - H_1(Rp, Y_1) = C' - C \qquad (4.9)$$

$$Y_1 - RC'' = C - C' \qquad (4.10)$$

$$Z + pM_1^s(p) = C'' \qquad (4.11)$$

where Y_1 is the value of the home output in terms of home currency, C' is the part of C allocated to foreigners and C'' is the value of C' in terms of the foreign currency. We can determine p, Y_1, E_1 and Z from (4.8), (4.9), (4.10) and (4.11) since R, C, C' and C'' are given, and know the changes in P, Y_1, E_1 and Z induced by a change in R.

As for the reason of the inflexibility of prices, Kemp mentioned, apart from the governmental control, oligopolistic pricing practices which may retard the response of prices to a change in demand.

This is very interesting, since fix-price models in recent disequilibrium theories are criticized that they fail to provide a rigorous theoretical justification of why prices are sticky (Cuddington [7]). In the case of repressed inflation, however, the oligopolistic price rigidity due to kinked demand curve seems to be irrelevant, since the reason for such rigidity is the existence of idle capacity in the sense that an increase in demand can be absorbed into an increase in output without any changes in prices (Sweezy [86]).

By assuming away the import competing industries, Kemp cleverly avoided the difficult problem of rationing of labor between industries in repressed inflation, which still remains unsolved, i.e., not explained by the optimizing behavior of economic agents in the recent literature on fixprice models (Cuddington [7]). As for the allocation of home-produced goods, Kemp's assumption that domestic demands have no priority is in contrast to that of Cuddington [7]. Because of this assumption, households of domestic consumers are constrained in the market for goods. Although Kemp considered carefully the possible effect of this constraint on forced savings, he dis not consider its effect on the supply of labor. When excess demand prevails in the market for home-produced goods, the excess may spill not only into savings (future consumption) bur also into leisure (reduction of labor supply), as well as into the market for the imported goods. Since a change in R induces a change in E_1, then, C cannot be assumed constant when we consider the effect of devaluation in (4.5)–(4.7) or (4.8)–(4.11). To take this effect into consideration fully, however, we have to wait for the later development of the theory of dual decisions in quantity constraint models by Clower [35] and Patinkin [75, p. 216].

Finally, Kemp implicitly assumed that gains from changes in the rate of exchange accrue entirely to the exporting country in the case of output allocation, which is recently followed by Cuddington [8]. Alternatively, of course, we may assume that the gains from foreign exchange accrue to the import distributors of the importing country (Negishi [20]).

5. QUANTITY CONSTRAINT MODELS OF A CLOSED ECONOMY

Studies in fix-price quantity constraint models were pioneered by Clower's [35] consideration of the dual decisions of households and

Patinkin's [75, chap. 13] consideration of those of firms. Notional demand for consumer goods and notional supply of factors of production are derived from the Walrasian model of households as functions of prices of goods and factors. When notional supply of factors of production is not realized, i.e., factor markets are in excess supply, households have to make dual decisions so as to have effective demand, since notional demand cannot be financed by the proceeds from the realized factor supply. Given the realized quantity of supply, then, effective demand is derived subject to budget constraints in which factor supplies are constrained by the realized quantities. They are functions not only of the prices of goods and factors but also of the realized income of households. While notional demand for labor is derived as a function of the real wage from the Walrasian model of the competitive firm, the effective demand for labor is constrained by the quantity of realized demand for output through the production function.

These models of dual decisions are generalized into fix-price quantity constraint general equilibrium models of a closed macro economy by, among others, Barro–Grossman [22], Benassy [24] and Malinvaud [15]. The quantity constraint model can be applied not only to the case of excess supply but also to the case of excess demand. An agent's supply in a market may be constrained by the fact that its notional demand in other markets is not fully satisfied. The supply of output by the firm is constrained by the availability of labor and other factors of production. Labor supply may be different when suppliers cannot spend as much of their income as they wish to obtain the consumer goods they want. In a non-tâtonnement economy in which trade occurs at Walrasian nonequilibrium prices, notional demand and supply are in general not fully realized. Demand or supply is rationed and some agents have to make transactions different from their notional demand of supply. Let us assume, however, that no agent is obliged to exchange more than it wants or in the other direction. It is reasonable then to assume the short-side principle that traders on the short side (i.e., suppliers if there is excess demand, demanders if there is excess supply) can realize their demand or supply fully. A trader on the longside of a market perceives a constraint, i.e., an upper bound on the trade he can realize in this particular market, which is given by the realized transaction. The effective demand and supply by agents in a market are derived, then, by utility or profit maximization,

and

$$L^s = L_0 - (a_3/a_2)(M_0/w) = L_3, \tag{5.8}$$

when the distribution of profit expected by consumer is

$$\Pi = pY^d - wL^s. \tag{5.9}$$

Corresponding to Y_2 and L_3, let us define L_2 and Y_3 by

$$Y_2 = F(L_2), \qquad Y_3 = F(L_3). \tag{5.10}$$

Disequilibrium combinations of real wages and real balance, i.e., w/p and M_0/p, are grouped as follows according to the sign of notional excess demand in the goods and labor markets.

I $Y^d - Y^s > 0,$ $L^d - L^s < 0,$

II $Y^d - Y^s < 0,$ $L^d - L^s < 0,$

III $Y^d - Y^s > 0,$ $L^d - L^s > 0,$

IV $Y^d - Y^s < 0,$ $L^d - L^s > 0.$

It is convenient to represent this in a $(M_0/p, w/p)$ diagram. In Figure 16, the real wage w/p is measured vertically and the real balance M_0/p horizontally.

The downward sloping curve L_1L_2 is the equilibrium locus of the goods market, which shows the different combinations of real wages

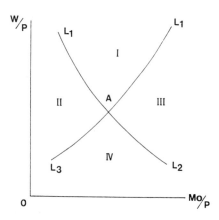

FIGURE 16   National equilibrium classification.

and real balance satisfying the condition $L_1 = L_2$. Since $F(L_1) = Y_1$ is the notional supply of the firm in (5.3) and $F(L_2) = Y_2$ is the notional demand of the consumer in (5.7) and (5.10), the condition $L_1 = L_2$ assures equilibrium in the goods market. This locus is downward sloping since L_1 is decreasing with respect to w/p in (5.3) where we assume diminishing marginal productivity while Y_2, and therefore L_2, is increasing with respect to M_0/p in (5.7). Any point above this curve corresponds to $L_2 > L_1$, which implies the existence of excess demand in the goods market, while any point below this curve corresponds to $L_2 < L_1$, which implies excess supply in the goods market.

Similarly, the curve L_1L_3 in Figure 16 shows the locus of the points corresponding to equilibrium in the labor market. The labor market is cleared if $L_1 = L_3$ since L_1 is the notional labor demand of the firm in (5.3) and L_3 is the notional supply of labor in (5.8). This locus is upward sloping since L_1 will be increased by a decrease in w/p from (5.3), while M_0/w must be reduced in (5.8) to maintain the equality of L_1 and L_3 which, in view of the decreasing w/p, requires a reduction in M_0/p. In view of (5.3) and (5.8), any point above this curve corresponds to $L_1 < L_3$, i.e., excess supply in the labor market, while any point below this curve corresponds to $L_1 > L_3$ which implies excess demand in the labor market.

In area I of Figure 16, there is notional excess demand in the goods market and excess supply in the labor market, which Benassy called stagflation. In area II, (III), excess supply (demand) prevails both in the goods market and labor market, i.e., deflation (inflation). Finally, in area IV we have excess demand in the labor market and excess supply in the goods market. If the law of demand and supply works in the sense of Walras, wages are bid up in areas III and IV and bid down in areas I and II. Similarly, prices are bid up in areas I and III while they are bid down in areas II and IV. Only at the point of intersection of the curves L_1L_2 and L_1L_3, i.e., point A, is Walrasian general equilibrium established and there are no changes in both p and w. If p and w are considered fixed, i.e., independent of excess demand and supply (Hicks [47, chap. 7]), however, all the points other than A can be made non-Walrasian equilibria by the introduction of quantity constraints on agents on the long side of markets, to which such agents adjust themselves through dual decisions.

When the situation in area I obtains, the firm is not constrained and the effective and notional demands (supplies) of the firm are identical since Y_1 and L_1 are realized according to the short-side principle. The consumer is, on the other hand, constrained and has to make dual decisions on demand in the goods market and on supply in the labor market, subject to the quantity constraint perceived in the other market.

The effective demand for output is obtained using the budget constraint

$$pY^d + M = M_0 + \pi + wL_1, \qquad (5.11)$$

since the consumer is now on the long side of the labor market and cannot sell more labor than L_1. The maximization of utility (5.2) with respect to Y_d and M, subject to (5.11), gives

$$\begin{aligned} Y^{de} &= (a_1/(a_1 + a_2))(M_0 + \pi + wL_1)/p \\ &= (a_1/(a_1 + a_2))((M_0/p) + Y_1), \end{aligned} \qquad (5.12)$$

in view of

$$\pi + wL_1 = pY_1. \qquad (5.13)$$

Since the effective supply of output Y^{se} is Y_1, the excess effective demand in the goods market in area I is

$$\begin{aligned} Y^{de} - Y^{se} &= (a_1/(a_1 + a_2))((M_0/p) + Y_1) - Y_1 \\ &= (a_2/(a_1 + a_2))(Y_2 - Y_1) \end{aligned} \qquad (5.14)$$

using (5.7) and (5.12).

Similarly, the effective supply of labor L^{se} is obtained using

$$M + w(L_0 - L^s) = M_0 + \pi + wL_0 - pY_1, \qquad (5.15)$$

in area I where the consumer is on the long side of the goods market and cannot buy more than Y_1. Maximizing (5.2) with respect to L^s and M, subject to (5.15), gives

$$L^{se} = L_0 - (a_3/(a_2 + a_3))(M_0 + \pi + wL_0 - pY_1)/w. \qquad (5.16)$$

Since the effective demand for labor L^{de} is L_1, the excess effective demand in the labor market in area I is

$$\begin{aligned} L^{de} - L^{se} &= L_1 - L_0 + (a_3/(a_2 + a_3))(M_0 + wL_0 + \pi - pY_1)/w \\ &= (a_2/(a_2 + a_3))(L_1 - L_3), \end{aligned} \qquad (5.17)$$

using (5.8), (5.13) and (5.16).

Since L_1 is the least among L_i in area I and therefore Y_1 is the least among Y_i in this area, effective excess supply exists in the labor market and effective excess demand in the goods market. The sign of the effective excess demand is, consequently, the same as the sign of notational excess demand in area I which Malinvaud [15] called Classical Unemployment.

In area II, notional supplies Y_1 and L_3 are not realized in both markets and therefore is expected that effective demand will not be greater than notional demand, with the sign of effective excess demand again unchanged by dual decisions. Since the firm is not to be constrained in the labor market, Y_1 remains the effective supply in the goods market. Since the consumer is constrained in the labor market, however, the effective demand for goods is again obtained using the budget constraint

$$pY^d + M = M_0 + \pi + wL, \tag{5.18}$$

where L is the realized employment. As a result of maximizing (5.2), this gives

$$Y^{de} = (a_1/(a_1 + a_2))((M_0/p) + Y) \tag{5.19}$$

in view of

$$\pi + wL = pY \tag{5.20}$$

where Y is the realized purchase of output. If the consumer is on the short side of the goods market, we should have

$$Y = Y^{de}. \tag{5.21}$$

From (5.7), (5.19) and (5.21), the effective demand for output in area II is

$$Y^{de} = (a_1/a_2)(M_0/p) = Y_2 \tag{5.22}$$

and therefore the excess effective demand for output is

$$Y^{de} - Y^{se} = Y_2 - Y_1 \tag{5.23}$$

in area II. In the labor market, on the other hand, the effective supply L^{se} coincides with the notional supply L_3 since the consumer is not to be constrained in the goods market and no dual decisions are made, if the fact that the expected distribution of the profit is not realized is ignored for the sake of simplicity. Effective demand in the labor market is, however, different from the notional demand since the firm is to be on the long side of the goods market. The firm must base its plan of demand for labor on realized sales in the goods market, which is Y_2 from (5.21) and (5.22), and therefore the effective demand for labor is L_2. Consequently the excess effective demand for labor is

$$L^{de} - L^{se} = L_2 - L_3. \qquad (5.24)$$

Since L_2 and Y_2 are, respectively, the least among L_i and Y_i and are therefore realized, excess effective supply dominates, as expected, both the labor and goods markets in area II.

In area III, notional demands Y_2 and L_1 are not realized in both markets and therefore effective supply is not expected to be greater than notional supply, with the sign of effective excess demand unchanged by dual decisions. Since the firm is on the short side of the goods market, the effective demand for labor is the same as the notional demand L_1. The consumer has, however, to make dual decisions on the supply of labor since it is constrained in the goods market. The effective supply of labor is again obtained by maximizing (5.2), subject to

$$M + w(L_0 - L^s) = M_0 + \pi + wL_0 - pY, \qquad (5.25)$$

where Y is the realized purchase of output. This gives

$$L^{se} = L_0 - (a_3/(a_2 + a_3))(M_0 + \pi + wL_0 - pY)/w. \qquad (5.26)$$

Since the consumer is on the short side of the labor market, the realized profit is

$$\pi = pY - wL^{se}. \qquad (5.27)$$

From (5.26) and (5.27), then, the effective supply of labor is

$$L^{se} = L_0 - (a_3/a_2)(M_0/w) = L_3, \qquad (5.28)$$

in view of (5.8). Therefore, the excess effective demand in the labor market is

$$L^{de} - L^{se} = L_1 - L_3. \qquad (5.29)$$

In the goods market, on the other hand, the effective demand Y^{de} coincides with the notional demand Y_2 since the consumer is not constrained in the labor market and there are no dual decisions to be considered, if we again ignore the fact that the expected profit is not realized. Effective supply in the goods market is, however, different from the notional supply since the firm is on the long side of the labor market and has to make dual decisions on the supply of output. The firm must base its plan of supply on the realized purchase of labor which is L_3 from (5.28). Therefore, the effective supply in the goods market is Y_3. Excess effective demand in the goods market is then

$$Y^{de} - Y^{se} = Y_2 - Y_3. \qquad (5.30)$$

Since L_3 and Y_3 are, respectively, the least among L_i and Y_i and therefore realized in area III, excess effective demand exists, as expected, in both the labor and goods markets.

Finally, in the case of area IV, the consumer is not constrained and makes no dual decisions with the result that effective demand in the goods market and effective supply in the labor market are the same as the notional ones, i.e., Y_2 and L_3. The firm is, on the other hand, constrained in both markets and dual decisions have to be made on demand in the labor market and on supply in the goods market. Effective demand in the labor market is L_2 since supply from the firm in the goods market is constrained at Y_2, and effective supply in the goods market is Y_3 since the demand from the firm in the labor market is constrained at L_3. Therefore, after making the dual decisions, the inequality between demand and supply in the two markets can be anything, depending on the relative magnitude of L_2 and L_3. Figure 17 is obtained from Figure 16 by adding L_2L_3 curve which shows the combination of w/p and M_0/p satisfying the condition that $L_2 = L_3$. This curve is upward sloping since L_2 is increased by an increase in M_0/p from (5.7), while M_0/w has to be reduced, from (5.8), and therefore w/p must be increased to keep L_3 equal to the increased L_2. Any point to the left of this curve satisfies the inequality $L_2 < L_3$ and any point to the right satisfies $L_2 > L_3$. In the subarea of area IV in Figure 16 which is located on the left of L_2L_3 in Figure 17, excess supply exists in both the labor and goods markets. Since the consumer is now constrained in the labor market and the firm is constrained in the goods market, we have (5.23) and (5.24) again as the results of further dual decisions. In Figure 17, therefore, area II is enlarged to include this subarea where effective excess demand is negative in both the labor market

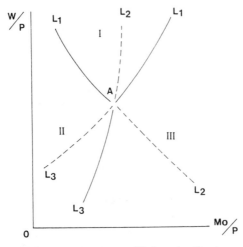

FIGURE 17   Effective equilibrium classification.

$(L_2 < L_3)$ and the goods market $(Y_2 < Y_1)$. This enlarged are II is
called Keynesian Unemployment by Malinvaud [15]. Similarly, in
the subarea of area IV located to the right of L_2L_3, excess demand
dominates both markets. Dual decisions repeated by the consumer
constrained in the goods market and the firm constrained in the
labor market imply (5.29) and (5.30) again, where effective demand
is positive in both goods market $(Y_2 > Y_3)$ and the labor market
$(L_1 > L_3)$. Therefore, area III is enlarged to include this subarea in
Figure 17. Malinvaud called this enlarged area III Repressed
Inflation. In Figure 17, area IV degenerates into a part of the curve
L_2L_3, i.e., AL_3.[21]

6. QUANTITY CONSTRAINT MODELS OF AN OPEN ECONOMY

6.1. Anticipations of quantity constraints

Before we discuss the recent applications of quantity constraint
models in international trade theory, it may be interesting and

---

[21] If utility and production functions are not well behaved, as was explicitly and/or
implicitly assumed, Figures 16 and 17 are either more complicated or degenerate.
See Hildenbrand [48]. See Ito [50] for further development of quantity constraint
models of a closed economy.

important to refer to two pioneering studies which anticipate and suggest such applications, since some of their suggestions have not been fully followed in recent studies.

Brito and Richardson [4] considered disequilibrium dynamics of exchange-rate changes and concluded that exchange-rate changes produce short-run perverse effects qualitatively opposite to their long-run effects. Proportional rates of increase in wages and the rate of inflation are assumed to be proportional to excess demands in the labor and commodity markets, respectively. When there is excess supply in the labor market, producers adjust employment proportionally to the difference between the desired demand for labor and actual employment, without regard to the current state of unemployment. When there is excess demand in the labor market, it is laborers who adjust employment proportionally to the difference between the desired supply of labor and actual employment, without regard to the current state of unfilled vacancies. In other words, the short-side principle prevails in the lagged quantity adjustment process in the labor market.

A reference is made to Clower [35] and Barro and Grossman [22], but strangely this is only for the assumption that wage-price adjustments are proportional to excess demands and not for dual decisions due to the short-side principle and quantity constraints. Desired demand for labor is simply assumed to be a function of the real wage only, i.e., the first postulate of the classical economics is adopted. Independent of their reference to Clower and Barro and Grossman, however, Brito and Richardson admitted that "the demand for labor in disequilibrium might be positively related to (perhaps cumulated) excess demand in commodity markets, as well as to labor's marginal product," referring to R. G. Lipsey's argument. Cumulated negative excess demand in commodity markets implies the existence of an inventory of unsold goods, which has not yet been taken into consideration in recent quantity constraint models. The desired supply of labor is assumed to be a function of the perceived real wage rate only and no consideration is given to possible dual decision of households facing excess demand in the market of domestic output. This is perhaps related to the fact that no distinction is made between desired real expenditure and actual real expenditure and the assumption that decisions on what to buy are determined after an overall spending-saving decision has been made, and independently of that overall decision. This may be defendable in the very short-run, but may not be so plausible in the longer run, unless domestically produced goods and imported goods are perfectly substitutable.

In his review of Frenkel and Johnson [42], *The Monetary Approach to the Balance of Payments,* Hahn [11] criticized Mundell to the effect that a system in which the price of nontraded goods adjusts slowly in response to excess demand is not a tâtonnement system, since trade out of equilibrium is to be carried out. In view of the relation between the non-tâtonnement system and quantity constraints (Negishi [73]), this is a suggestion that quantity constraint models should be used in disequilibrium analysis of international trade. As we shall see, this suggestion was followed by Liviatan [14], one of the recent applications of quantity constraint models in international trade theory.

Hahn also raised questions concerning the small country assumption in international trade theory, which seems to assume away the quantity constraints. Mundell and other authors of Frenkel and Johnson [42] assumes that the home country can sell to the world at the going price whatever it wishes to, because home country is small. Hahn finds this assumption about the export market far-fetched, although export prices may indeed have to be taken as given. "While there may be a world price for family cars, this does not mean that British Leyland can sell to the Germans whatever they like at that price. It only means that they cannot charge more without losing most of their customers or charge less without strong retaliations." This is really an important suggestion since, as we shall see, the quantity constraints on demand for exportables of the home country is assumed away in the case of small country by Liviatan who followed Hahn in other respects as well as by others in recent studies on quantity constraint models.

6.2. Constraints in labor market

We can find in Dixit [9] an example of the earliest and simplest applications of quantity constraint models in the theory of international economy. Dixit points out the poor choice theoretical framework of the conventional income-expenditure approach which is embodied in the diagrams of Swan [85] and Mundell [67]. Nor is he satisfied with the monetary approach of Frenkel and Johnson [42], which assumes instantaneous attainment of Walrasian equilibrium in commodity and labor markets. His aim is to develop a more satisfactory approach to the problem of the balance of trade by a fixprice non-Walrasian model of temporary equilibrium, based on a dual decision approach like those of Barro and Grossman [22] and Malinvaud [15]. The model is very similar to the one we have explained for the case of a closed economy (in Section 5), with only one aggregate commodity, one type of labor, and fiat money, but no other assets. Actually, it is made simpler in two ways. Firstly, it is assumed that the profits earned by the producer in a period do not accrue to the consumer as income in the same period. Secondly, there is no need for any rationing in the commodity market, since any discrepancy between domestic output and demand simply shows up as exports or imports, which can be always realized for a small country.

Consider a small country in short-run equilibrium with a given money supply $\bar{m}$, wage rate w, and price level p. Since the foreign price level is assumed to be fixed, p is given if the exchange rate is given. When there are no quantity constraints, the aggregate notional commodity supply and labor demand of the competitive producers are given as $y = \pi_p(p, w)$ and $e = -\pi_w(p, w)$ by partial differentiation with respect to p and w of the profit function $\pi(p, w)$ which is increasing in p, decreasing in w, and convex and homogeneous of degree one in p and w (Varian [88, pp. 30–31]). The notional demands for the commodity and for money and the notional supply of labor of the aggregate consumer are $x(p, w, m)$, $m(p, w, \bar{m})$ and $l(p, w, \bar{m})$, which are obtained by utility maximization under a budget constraint,

$$px + m = wl + \bar{m}.$$

The clearance of the labor market requires

$$l(p, w, \bar{m}) + \pi_w(p, w) = 0 \qquad (6.1)$$

which corresponds to the curve FE in Figure 18. To see that this curve is upward-sloping, differentiate (6.1) to obtain

$$dw/dp = -(l_p + \pi_{wp})/(l_w + \pi_{ww}) \qquad (6.2)$$

where l_p is the partial differentiation of l with respect to p, π_{ww} is the partial differentiation of π_w with respect to w, and the like. We know from the properties of π that π_{ww} is positive. By ruling out a backward-bending labor supply curve, Dixit assumed that $l_w > 0$. If l_p is negative, then, the right-hand side of (6.2) is positive and the curve FE in Figure 18 is upward-sloping.

To show that l_p is negative, Dixit used skillfully the constrained demand for commodity $x'(p, w, e, \bar{m})$, i.e., the demand for the commodity in the case where the consumer must accept employment at the level e determined by the demand for labor of the producer. This is obtained by the maximization of utility with respect to x' and m', subject to the budget constraint, $px' + m' = we + m$. Since the constrained effective demand x' and the notional demand x coincide if the rationed amount of employment e happens to equal the desired notional labor supply,

$$x(p, w, \bar{m}) = x'(p, w, l(p, w, \bar{m}), \bar{m}). \tag{6.3}$$

Differentiation of (6.3) with respect to p yields

$$x_p = x'_p + x'_e l_p \tag{6.4}$$

where x'_e denotes the partial differentiation of x' with respect to e and the like. Dixit assumed that x'_e is positive and both x_p and x'_p are negative, by ruling out inferiority. Now the LeChatelier–Samuelson Principle (Samuelson [78]) suggests that the demand for a commodity becomes less price elastic when some other commodity is rationed.[22] Therefore, $-x_p > -x'_p > 0$, and $l_p < 0$, from (6.4).

Next consider the surplus in the balance of trade, measured in units of the aggregate commodity, i.e. the difference between domestic production and demand, $s = y - x$. If we consider the notational trade balance, ignoring the dual decisions caused by constraints in the labor market,

$$s = \pi_p(p, w) - x(p, w, \bar{m}) \tag{6.5}$$

---

[22] This is, however, not necessarily the case when the substitution effect is relatively smaller than the income effect, as one can easily see by drawing a figure like Figure 15. Samuelson [77, p. 168] carefully applied LeChatelier principle only to the case of a compensated change in price. We owe valuable suggestions to Professors Y. Kimura of Nagoya City University, K. Kiyono of Gakushuin University, and S. Kusumoto of Tsukuba University.

and the slope of the curve $s = 0$ (BT in Figure 18) is

$$dw/dp = (\pi_{pp} - x_p)/(-\pi_{pw} + x_w).\tag{6.6}$$

Dixit assumed that x_p is negative while π_{pp} and $-\pi_{pw}$ are positive. To consider the sign of x_w differentiate (6.3) with respect to w,

$$x_w = x'_w + x'_e l_w\tag{6.7}$$

where x'_e and l_w are positive. Since inferiority is ruled out and employment is fixed at e, x'_w is positive, so that x_w is also positive from (6.7). Therefore, the right-hand side of (6.6) is positive and the curve BT is positively sloped in Figure 18.

The notional equilibrium classification is shown in Figure 18 where regions are labelled U for unemployment (excess supply of labor), E for excess demand for labor, S for trade surplus and D for deficit (negative s). The curves are FE for full employment and BT for balanced trade, and their intersection is the short-run Walrasian equilibrium. Dixit assumed that the curve BT is steeper than the curve FE and justified the assumption by arguing that low wage and price levels have a favorable real balance effect on demand, i.e., E and D are in the region to the south-west of W.

The notional equilibrium classification must, however, be converted into an effective equilibrium classification for, in the region U, s should be defined not as (6.5) but as

$$s = \pi_p(p, w) - x'(p, w, -\pi_w(p, w), \bar{m})\tag{6.8}$$

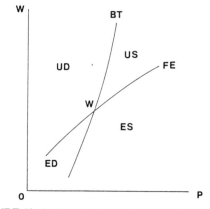

FIGURE 18   Notional balance of trade and employment.

since the consumer is constrained in the labor market and has to make a dual decision, while in the region E, s should be defined as

$$s = F(l(p, w, \bar{m})) - x(p, w, \bar{m}) \qquad (6.9)$$

where F is the production function of the producer, since the producer is constrained in the labor market and the employment is determined by the supply of labor. By assuming that utility and production functions are of the Cobb–Douglas (i.e., log-linear) type, Dixit obtained the fixprice effective equilibrium classification of Figure 19.

Both the strength and the weakness of Dixit's model lie in the simplifying assumption that there is no constraint in the commodity market. Comparative statics studies are made for the effects of three parameter changes. Firstly, an increase in the money supply $\bar{m}$ shifts the FE curve upward and the BT curve to the right. More rigorously, new curves are a radial enlargement of the old ones. With w and p sticky, the economy initially located at W is now in the ED region relative to new curves. Unlike in the case of a closed economy, however, there is a further change in m, i.e., a gradual reduction of $\bar{m}$ below its initially increased value due to the trade deficit at W. The effective equilibrium curves begin to shrink back and the Walrasian equilibrium drifts radially back towards W.

Secondly, Dixit considered a fiscal policy, i.e., the case where the government acts by purchasing an amount g of the commodity. The

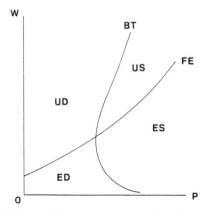

FIGURE 19   Effective balance of trade and employment.

trade surplus is now $s = y - x - g$ and the curve BT shifts to the right while FE is unaltered. The impact effect is a rise in the trade deficit, with no change in the state of the labor market. This is formally the same result as that attributed to the so-called New Cambridge School that any increase in the government deficit has to be reflected in an equal increase in the trade deficit. Dixit tried to spell out conditions responsible for this extreme case i.e., the assumption of sticky prices including exchange rate, neglect of the role of non-tradables, and that of the effect of taxes. We may add, however, that more important is the basic assumption that there is no quantity constraint in the commodity market, since as Hahn [11] suggests it is a different assumption from the assumption of sticky price.

Finally, effects of an upward shift in productivity are considered. The FE curve is shifted upward while the BT curve is shifted to the left, so that the economy initially at Walrasian equilibrium is now in the ES region. This is in contrast to Malinvaud's [15] result that in a closed economy the impact effect of a productivity increase is Keynesian unemployment. There is no room for Keynesian unemployment in Dixit's model, since "the extra output can be sold abroad at the going world price" and an upward shift in productivity does not face the problem of generating enough commodity demand. Dixit thinks that his picture is more realistic than Malinvaud's for most countries, and Germany is an obvious example. We really hope that Dixit is right and that people do not blame Japanese exports for unemployment in most countries. Dixit concluded that his model is capable of encompassing the essential features of both the Keynes–Meade and the monetary approaches. As we have seen (in Section 4.1), the Keynes–Meade model is not truly Keynesian in the sense that unemployment there is not a typically Keynesian one due to the deficiency of effective demand for commodities. What is left to be done may be the introduction of non-traded goods, as Dixit himself admitted. Alternatively we may consider, as Hahn suggested, the quantity constraints in the commodity market even in the case of small countries.

6.3. Introduction of non-traded goods

Non-traded goods are introduced in Chan's model [6]. The economy is divided into two sectors: an export sector producing only for export, and a non-traded good sector. Consumers consume the non-traded good and an imported good which is not produced at home. The price of exports and imports are exogenously determined in terms of foreign currency, but a small country does not face quantity constraints in the export and import markets. The non-traded good market and the foreign exchange market are cleared very rapidly since the price of the non-traded good and the free exchange rate adjust very quickly. Given a rigid money wage set above the market clearing level, however, the labor market fails to clear, inducing involuntary unemployment.

Although non-traded goods are introduced, therefore, unemployment considered is not typically a Keynesian one, since producers are not constrained, either in the export market or in the non-traded good market, by insufficient demand. Chan's interest was to show that an increase in the tariff unambiguously reduces aggregate employment.[23] Das [38] followed Chan and argued that Chan's result crucially depends on the assumption that labor is the only mobile factor. He considered the Heckscher–Ohlin model with a linear-homogeneous production function, introducing another mobile factor whose market is cleared continuously. This implies the shift from short-run stabilization problem of a macro economy to a long-run allocation problem such as we considered in Sections 1 through 3.

Liviatan [14] considered the case where domestic price and wage rates are not fully flexible. His model consists of traded goods, non-traded goods, money and labor. The assumption of a small country and fixed exchange rates enables him to make the price of traded goods constant.

The price of the non-traded good in terms of the traded good is denoted by p and the domestic money supply in terms of foreign currency is denoted by m. If the clearance of the labor market by a flexible wage is assumed and, unlike Dixit [9] and Neary [18], the profit of firms are assumed to be distributed to households instantaneously, Walras's law holds as

$$E_T(p, m) + pE_N(p, m) + E_m(p, m) = 0 \qquad (6.10)$$

where E_T, E_N and E_m denote, respectively, excess demand for

---

[23] See Cuddington–Johansson–Lofgren [36, chap. 7] for further details.

traded goods, that for non-traded good, excess demand for domestic money expressed in terms of foreign currency.

Assuming gross substitution, i.e., $(\partial E_N/\partial p)$ and $(\partial E_m/\partial m)$ are negative while all other partials are positive, Liviatan derived the shapes of the two curves of Figure 20, where the NN' curve corresponds to $E_N = 0$ and mm' curve corresponds to $E_m = 0$. The relative positions of NN' and mm' follows from Walras' law, i.e., the absolute value of $p(\partial E_N/\partial p)$ is larger than $(\partial E_m/\partial p)$ and the absolute value of $(\partial E_m/\partial m)$ is larger than $p(\partial E_N/\partial m)$, so that mm' is steeper than NN'.

If p is flexible and clears the market for non-traded goods, the economy is located on the curve NN'. Since a trade surplus increases the money supply, we have

$$dm/dt = -E_T = E_m, \qquad t = \text{time} \qquad (6.11)$$

from Walras' law. The convergence to Q on NN' can be easily seen, since E_m is negative to the right of mm' and positive to the left of mm'.

Liviatan first considers the case where p is not fully flexible but the labor market is continuously cleared by a fully flexible wage, and argues that the effects of disequilibrium in the non-traded good market must be taken into consideration to analyze the changes in p and m, following Hahn's [11] criticism of Mundell. In Figure 20, the region located above NN' is denoted D and that located below it is

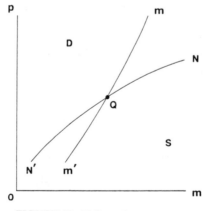

FIGURE 20   Full employment case.

denoted by S. In the former region, there exists an excess supply in the non-traded good market and actual production is determined by demand, while in the latter region there exists an excess demand and supply determines actual production.

In D, the effective national product $I'(p, m)$ is smaller than the notional national product $I(p, m)$, since the notional supply of the non-traded good $N_S(p)$ cannot be realized and the production of the non-traded good is constrained by demand which is smaller than supply, even though the effective supply of the traded good is increased by the shift of resources from the production of the non-traded good. The effective demand for the non-traded good $N'_d(p, I', m)$, therefore, is smaller than the notional demand for non-traded good $N_d(p, I, m)$ which is by definition smaller than $N_S(p)$. Similarly, the effective excess demand for money $E'_m(p, I', m)$ is smaller than the notional excess demand for money $E_m(p, I, m)$ and the relevant portion of the effective equilibrium curve for m, mQ, must lie to the left of the corresponding notional equilibrium curve, except at Q.

Since the supply of the non-traded good is forced into equality with demand in D, $E'_m(p, I', m) + E'_T(p, I', m) = 0$ is an identity. In other words, the effective desired change in money balance E'_m is identical to the actual change in money supply or trade surplus (deficit, if negative), i.e., $-E'_T$. When the production of the non-traded good is governed by demand, an increase in p reduces the production of non-traded good through decreased demand and releases factors of production to produce more of the traded good and thus improve the balance of payments. If this production effect of an increase in p on the traded good dominates the demand substitution effect which leads to a negative effect on the balance of trade, E'_m is, like E_m, an increasing function of p and the slope of mQ is positive.

Turning to the supply determined region S, Liviatan finds that the effective and notional incomes coincide here. By assuming that consumers consider the quantity constraint on the non-traded good to be permanent so that the excess demand for the stock of money is not affected much, he concludes that the Qm' portion of the mm' curve is not much different from the notional equilibrium one in the case of perfectly flexible p.

To the right of the mm' curve m is reduced by the trade deficit, while to the left of the mm' curve m is increased by the trade surplus. As for the dynamic behavior of p, it increases in S and decreases in D. Liviatan describes the latter dynamic system as

$$
\begin{aligned}
dp/dt &= a_D(N_d'(p, m) - N_s(p)) && \text{in } D \\
dp/dt &= a_S E_N(p, m) && \text{in } S
\end{aligned}
\tag{6.12}
$$

where a_i is a speed of adjustment parameter in region i. Liviatan called $N_d' - N_s$ in D and E_N in S the potential excess demand for the non-traded good, which others may call effective excess demand. The reason is that effective excess demand for non-traded good is, according to Liviatan, taken to be identically zero. This little confusion suggests to us that further studies are necessary on how prices are changed, or not changed, in disequilibrium.

The second case considered by Liviatan is the one where the real wage is not fully flexible so that the labor market is out of equilibrium, but the non-traded good market is cleared by a fully flexible p. The real wage in terms of the tradables is denoted by w and the demand for labor in the non-traded good sector L_N is assumed to be a decreasing function of w/p, while that in the traded good sector L_T is assumed to be a decreasing function of w. The equilibrium wage which equates the total demand for labor $L_N + L_T$ with inelastic total labor supply is a function of p and denoted by $\bar{w}$. If $w > \bar{w}$, we have unemployment, while we have excess demand for labor or overemployment if $w < \bar{w}$. In the latter situation there is the question of how the labor supply is rationed among the sectors. Liviatan assumes that for all $w < \bar{w}$ the allocation of labor is according to the equilibrium wage $\bar{w}$. In other words, the allocation of labor remains unchanged for $w < \bar{w}$ if p and $\bar{w}$ do not change.

If w is flexible, the labor market can be cleared. Since an increase in m increases p and an increase in p increases $\bar{w}$, m and w are positively related for the clearance of the labor market, as is shown in the LL' curve of Figure 21. In the region D above LL' we have unemployment and w decreases, while in the region S below LL' we have overemployment and w increases. Employment is determined by the demand for labor in D and by the supply of labor in S.

To analyze the behavior of m, consider first the D region. Effective income is given by

$$
I'(w, p) = T_s(w) + p N_s(w/p)
\tag{6.13}
$$

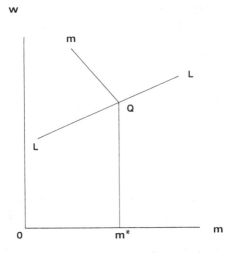

FIGURE 21   Unemployment and overemployment.

where T_s and N_s denote the supplies of traded and non-traded good
sectors, since actual employment in both sectors is given by the
corresponding demand functions L_T and L_N. Since the non-traded
good market has to be cleared,

$$N_s(w/p) = N_d(p, I'(w, p), m) \tag{6.14}$$

where N_d signifies the demand for the non-traded good. From
(6.14), we can solve p as a function of w and m, say $p = p(w, m)$.
While it can be shown that p is increasing with respect to m, to
show that p is increasing with respect to w we have to assume that
the upward cost push effect of w on p dominates the downward
demand pull effect due to $(\partial I'/\partial w) < 0$.

Since households are forced to adjust their labor supply to the
demand for labor and the non-traded good market is cleared, the
effective desired excess demand for money E'_m is identical to the
effective trade surplus $-E'_T$ which implies actual increase in m.
Since

$$E'_T(w, m) = T_d(p(w, m), I'(w, p(w, m)), m) - T_s(w) \tag{6.15}$$

where T_d denotes demand for the traded good, we can show that E'_m
is decreasing with respect to m. An increase in w has a negative

effect on trade balance because it pushes p upward which generates an adverse substitution effect. On the other hand, an increase in w increases unemployment and reduces income, which generates a favorable income effect on the trade balance. Assuming the cost the push effect is dominant, Liviatan concluded that E'_m is also decreasing with respect to w. It then follows that the $E'_m = 0$ curve in D is downward sloping like mQ in Figure 21. To the right of the curve mQ, m decreases, and, to the left of it, m increases.

Turning to the overemployment region S, let us recall that the allocation of labor is according to $\bar{w}$ which is a function of p, say $\bar{w}$ (p). The equilibrium condition for the non-traded good market can be used to determine p as a function of m, say $p = g(m)$, since the supply of the non-traded good is a function of p only. Both $\bar{w}$ and p are functions of m alone and so is E'_T. As in Figure 21, the equilibrium curve $E'_m = 0$ in S is represented by a vertical line through m^* which can be obtained from $E'_T = 0$. To the right of Qm^*, m decreases, and, to the left of it, m increases, since an increase in m raises p which raises income so that E'_T is an increasing function of m.

In comparison with Dixit [9] and Neary [18], one of the main features of Liviatan [14] lies in a detailed analysis of dynamics in disequilibria. Liviatan skillfully argued that the convergence is non-cyclical in the case where p is not fully flexible and that a monetary expansion creates an employment cycle with overemployment being followed by unemployment in the case where w is not fully flexible. Although the distinction is made between tradables and nontradables, which Dixit neglected, nevertheless, some problems remain. Firstly, the traded good sector does not face a demand constraint while the non-traded good sector does. In other words, exporting industries can always enjoy enough demand even if industries producing for the domestic market face a deficiency of demand. Although such a case may be possible in a particular historical situation, as in the U.K. in 1930's, there is no theoretical reason why such is always the case even for a small country, as Hahn [11] suggested. Secondly, Liviatan considered constraints in the labor market and in the non-traded good market separately. It is necessary to consider these constraints jointly, which is a task left to be done by Neary [18].

6.4. Constraints in labor and non-traded good markets

Extending Dixit [9] by adding a non-traded good whose price is sticky, Neary [19] skillfully discussed the relationship between different regimes due to different combinations of disequilibria both in labor and non-traded good markets, i.e., Classical Unemployment, Keynesian Unemployment, Repressed Inflation, etc. This is the first full-scale application of quantity constraint models of a closed economy (explained in Section 5) to international trade. His model consists of a non-traded good whose price is p_1, traded good whose price is p_2, labor whose wage is w and money. The small country assumption and given exchange rate enable him to make p_2 constant, and it is assumed that firms and households are never constrained in traded good markets. Following Dixit he assumes that profits are distributed to consumers in the next period and do not directly affect consumption decisions.

Let us start with his notional labor market equilibrium locus ($LMEL$) and notional nontraded good market equilibrium locus ($NTEL$) shown in Figure 22. $LMEL$ is given by

$$l(p_1, p_2, w, I) = e_1(p_1, w, h) + e_2(p_2, w, k) \qquad (6.16)$$

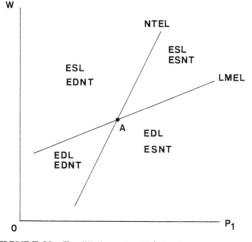

FIGURE 22   Equilibrium classification in open economy.

where l is the notional or unconstrained labor supply, e_1 is the notional or unconstrained demand for labor for the production of the non-traded good, e_2 is that for the production of the traded good, I is the lump-sum income consisting of money balances carried over from the past, transfer payments received from the government, divided payments (the last period's profit), and h and k are parameters representing the state of technology. *NTEL* is given by

$$y_1(p_1, w, h) = x_1(p_1, p_2, w, I) + g_1 \qquad (6.17)$$

where y_1 is the notional or unconstrained supply of the non-traded good, x_1 is the notional or unconstrained demand for the non-traded good, and g_1 is the government purchase of the non-traded good.

With gross substitutability in demand, both of these loci are upward-sloping in $w - p_1$ space, i.e., Figure 22. For example, starting from a point on *LMEL*, an increase in the wage will lead to excess supply of labor, requiring an increase in p_1 to restore equilibrium. Excess supply of labor (*ESL*) prevails in the region above *LMEL* and excess demand for labor (*EDL*) exists in the region below *LMEL*. The non-traded good market is in excess demand (*EDNT*) to the left of *NTEL* while it is in excess supply (*ESNT*) to the right of *NTEL*. The relative position of *LMEL* and *NTEL* is justified, either by Dixit [9]'s argument that the region of excess demand in both markets should correspond to low rather than high values of w and p_1 in view of real-balance effects or by Liviatan's [14] argument based on homogeneity and gross substitutability.

Neary then turns to consider the case where w and p_1 are assumed to be completely fixed within the current period. Any point in Figure 22, not just A, is now a short-run or temporary equilibrium. But at all points other than A, at least one market is to be cleared by quantity rationing, and this affects decisions in other markets according to Clower's dual decision hypothesis. In particular, the two equilibrium loci and hence the partitioning of $w - p_1$ space into different regions are affected.

Consider *NTEL* under excess supply of labor, i.e., in the *ESL* region above *LMEL* in Figure 22. When there is excess supply of labor but the non-traded good market is in equilibrium, non-traded good firms are not constrained in any market and their effective supply function remains their notional one. However, households are constrained to supply less labor than they wish to and their notional demand function for non-traded good $x_1(p_1, p_2, w, I)$ must be replaced by a constrained demand function. *NTEL* becomes in *ESL*

$$y_1(p_1, w, h) = x_1'(\bar{l}(p_1, p_2, w, h, k), p_1, p_2, w, I) + g_1 \quad (6.18)$$

where

$$\bar{l}(p_1, p_2, w, h, k) = e_1(p_1, w, h) + e_2(p_2, w, k) \quad (6.19)$$

and x_1' is the constrained demand for the non-traded good when the supply of labor is rationed to $\bar{l}$. Since $\bar{l}$ is less than the notional labor supply l, which is larger than the right hand side of (6.19), in *ESL*, x_1' must be less than the notional demand x_1. Thus, any point on the old *NTEL* located above *LMEL* (dotted curves in Figure 23) yields excess supply of the non-traded good, as is seen from the comparison of (6.17) and (6.18). In Figure 23 *NTEL* must be rotated around A to *NTEL* (*ESL*) so that the region K of generalized excess supply (*ESL–ESNT* in Figure 22) expands when

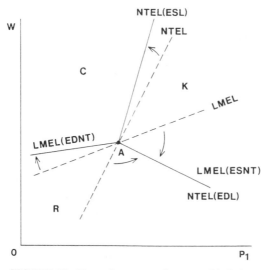

FIGURE 23 Unemployment and repressed inflation.

we move from considering notional to considering effective equilibria.

Turning next to *NTEL* under excess demand, i.e., in the *EDL* region below *LMEL*, Neary first assumes that the traded good sector has priority in the labor market and is not constrained even if labor is in excess demand. The non-traded good sector can employ only the total labor supply less the traded good sector's notional labor demand. *NTEL* in *EDL* becomes

$$F(l(p_1, p_2, w, I) - e_2(p_2, w, k), h) = x_1(p_1, p_2, w, I) + g_1 \quad (6.20)$$

where F is the production function of non-traded good. The left hand side is the non-traded good sector's employment-constrained supply function, which is less than its notional supply y_1. From the comparison of (6.17) and (6.20), therefore, any point on old *NTEL* in *EDL* yields an excess demand for the non-traded good. *NTEL* must be rotated around A to *NTEL(EDL)* so that the region R of *EDL–EDNT* is enlarged.

What is interesting is that (6.20) corresponds also to *LMEL* in *ESNT* where firms must produce less than their notional supply of non-traded good and their effective demand for labor is given by the inverse of the production function,

$$l(p_1, p_2, w, I) = F^{-1}(x_1(p_1, p_2, w, I) + g_1, h) + e_2(p_2, w, k). \quad (6.21)$$

Since the constrained demand for labor is less than the notional one, any point on the old *LMEL* in the right of *NTEL* yields an excess supply of labor, so that the region K of excess supply in both markets must be expanded by rotating *LMEL* around A to *LMEL(ESNT)* which coincides with *NTEL(EDL)* since (6.21) is identical with (6.20). The region of *ESNT–EDL* vanishes as in the case of a closed economy under the same assumption that commodity stock cannot be carried over to the next period and firms' decisions are of a one-period nature.

Finally, in *EDNT* households are unable to obtain as much non-traded good as they wish and they adjust their labor supply, taking the goods market constraint into account. *LMEL* in *EDNT* is given by

$$l'(\bar{x}_1(p_1, w, h, g_1), p_1, p_2, w, I) = e_1(p_1, w, h)$$
$$+ e_2(p_2, w, k) \quad (6.22)$$

where the constrained consumption of the non-traded good is what is left over after the government makes its priority purchases,

$$\bar{x}_1(p_1, w, h, g_1) = y_1(p_1, w, h) - g_1 \qquad (6.23)$$

and l' is the constrained supply of labor when the demand for the non-traded good is rationed to $\bar{x}_1$. Assuming that l' is increasing with respect to $\bar{x}_1$, we may conclude that any point on the old $LMEL$ in $EDNT$, i.e., to the left of $NTEL$, yields excess demand for labor, from the comparison of (6.16) with (6.22), since $\bar{x}_1$ is less than x_1. $LMEL$ must be rotated around A to $LMEL(ENDT)$ so that the region R of general excess demand is enlarged.

If the traded good sector has priority in the excess demanded labor market, therefore, we have three regions in Figure 23, labeled C for Classical Unemployment (households are rationed in both the excess supplied labor and the excess demanded non-traded good markets), K for Keynesian Unemployment (households are rationed in the excess supplied labor market, non-traded good firms are constrained in the excess supplied output market) and R for Repressed Inflation (households are constrained in the excess demanded non-traded good markets, and non-traded good firms are rationed in the excess demanded labor market). If the non-traded good sector is given priority in labor allocation when there is an excess demand for labor, however, we have the fourth region labeled U (for Underconsumption) in Figure 24, where the non-traded good firms are unconstrained in the excess demanded labor market but rationed in the excess supplied goods market, and traded good firms which are assumed to be unconstrained in the goods market are rationed in the excess demanded labor market. This is because the effective $NTEL$ in EDL is given by (6.17) and coincides with the notional $NTEL$ below $LMEL$. This result is interesting, since the fourth region is impossible in the case of a closed economy, unless firms have a two or more period horizon (Malinvaud [15, appendix], Meullbauer and Portes [66]).

Neary derived many interesting results in comparative statics. Naturally those are hybrids of the results obtained by Dixit [9] who assumed away the non-traded good and those obtained by Malinvaud [15] who considered the case of a closed economy. Consider, for example, the effects of technical progress, assuming that it increases the demand for labor at a given wage and price. They

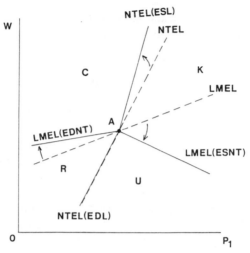

FIGURE 24   The case of underconsumption.

differ greatly depending on whether progress takes place in the traded or the non-traded good sector (whether k or h changes). In the former case, excess demand for labor appears at the old Walrasian equilibrium A, as was insisted by Dixit. By contrast, starting at Walrasian equilibrium, technical progress in the non-traded sector leads to Keynesian unemployment, as was insisted by Malinvaud. Similarly for the effects on employment of a wage cut. Since profits are assumed not to be consumed, a wage cut in region K reduces employment in a closed economy through its depressing effect on aggregate demand, whereas in Dixit's open economy a wage cut always increases output and employment. Neary found both of these effects in his model, the former applying to the non-traded good sector and the latter to the traded good sector, the net effect depending on the relative strengths of these two effects.

While expansionary fiscal and monetary policies (increases in g_1, g_2, and I) almost always worsen the trade balance, the effect of a devaluation (an increase in p_2) is not unambiguous even for a small country. In region K, for example, the trade surplus is given as

$$s = y_2(p_2, w, k) - x_2'(\bar{l}, p_1, p_2, w, I) - g_2 \qquad (6.24)$$

where y_2 is the supply of the traded good, x_2' is the constrained demand for the traded good when the supply of labor is rationed to

$\bar{l}$, and g_2 is the government purchase of the traded good. The level of employment $\bar{l}$ is given by the solution of

$$\bar{l} = F^{-1}(x_1'(\bar{l}, p_1, p_2, w, I) + g_1, h) + e_2(p_2, w, k) \qquad (6.25)$$

since in region K employment is demand-constrained; but the demand for labor of the non-traded good firms depends on the sales constraint that they face, and this sales constraint in turn depends on the employment constraint facing households through the x_1' function. From (6.24) and (6.25), we can compute $(\partial s/\partial p_2)$. While the devaluation improves the trade balance through the direct price effects in increasing the supply of and reducing the home demand for the traded good, there is an additional effect that could worsen the trade balance. The devaluation increases the demand for the non-traded good, so relaxing the goods market constraint facing the non-traded good sector. The resulting expansion in employment could lead to a sufficiently large increase in spending on the traded good to offset the direct price effects and worsen the trade balance.

Taking also into consideration the findings that devaluation affects employment in regions C and K more predictably than do fiscal and monetary policy, Neary concluded that his model gives some support to the policy assignment associated with the New Cambridge school, fiscal policy for external balance, exchange rate policy for internal balance. Taken in conjunction with the argument of Dixit [9], this suggests that what is ultimately responsible for this policy assignment is not the absence of a non-traded good but the assumption of a small country in the sense that the first postulate of classical economics holds in the traded good sector.

7. ASSESSMENT OF QUANTITY CONSTRAINT MODELS

7.1. The assumption of a small country

In the quantity constraint models of international trade that we have reviewed so far, the assumption of a small country is made so that the price is fixed and no one is constrained in the traded goods market. In other words, it is assumed that people can buy or sell whatever amount of good they wish to as far as the traded good is concerned. On account of this assumption, the models are essentially no more complicated than the case of the closed economy, even if a non-traded good is introduced (Neary [18]). An attempt is made, however, by Cuddington [7] to discard this powerful simplifying assumption.

In contrast to Dixit's [9] model, which has a single traded good market which always clears due to the small country assumption, Cuddington's [7] model has two output sectors, "an important generalization for trade models," and non-market-clearing situations are emphasized for one of the traded goods. In the market for the exportable good, the possibility of world excess demand or supply is admitted, while the economy is small in the market for importable goods and any domestic excess demand can always be satisfied by imports. Since the importable good may be in excess supply so that it is actually exported, Cuddington even argued that the important distinction between the exportable and importable goods is that the small country assumption applies for the latter but not the former. By assuming away the non-traded good, Cuddington can still talk of classical unemployment, Keynesian unemployment and repressed inflation, by considering non-market-clearing in the labor and exportable good markets.

Cuddington [8]'s aim is to demonstrate in detail that increases in government expenditure and exchange rate depreciation have quite different effects on output and employment as well as exports and imports depending on the type of market imbalance prevailing at the time of the policy change. We have to be satisfied, however, with a mere sketch of his model in the case of Keynesian unemployment where export is constrained quantitatively, a new situation considered by Cuddington, and in the case of repressed inflation where Cuddington gave an interesting argument concerning the allocation of labor between the export and import competing sectors.

Keynesian unemployment is characterized by excess supply both in the labor and the exportable good markets. The level of output of the exportable good Y_x' is determined by the sum of domestic and foreign demand for it,

$$Y_x' = D_x(p, e, Z') + X^d(p, e) + G_x < Y_x^s(L_x^d(w/p)) \qquad (7.1)$$

where D_x is the domestic private demand for the exportable good, X^d is the foreign demand for the exportable good, G_x is the government demand for the exportable good, Y_x^s is the domestic output of the exportable good, L_x^d is the notional demand for labor in the exportable good sector, p is the fixed price of the exportable good, e is the fixed exchange rate, identified with the domestic currency price of the importable good, w is the fixed nominal wage, and Z' is the consumption expenditure.

Because of the small country assumption, the domestic importables production Y_m^s is given by

$$Y_m^s = Y_m^s(L_m^d(w/e)) \tag{7.2}$$

where L_m^d is the notional demand for labor in the importable good sector. Nominal GNP is consequently limited by the demand for the exportable good,

$$Y' = pY_x' + eY_m^s. \tag{7.3}$$

Following Kemp [57, pp. 277–281] and Chan [6], Cuddington considered that the current consumption expenditure is a function of the disposable income $Y - T$ and wealth W only and prices do not affect it except through their effect on income. This is because households are assumed to regard all changes in prices as permanent, tastes do not change through time, and the utility function relating present and future consumption is assumed to be homothetic. Then Z' in (7.1) is given by

$$Z' = Z'(Y' - T, W). \tag{7.4}$$

In the Keynesian unemployment case the first postulate of classical economics does not hold in the exportable good sector and the effective demand for labor L_x' is derived from the demanded level of output Y_x' by reference to the production function. Total employment therefore equals

$$L = L_x'(Y_x') + L_m^d(w/e) < L^s(w/p, W/P) \tag{7.5}$$

where L^s is the notional supply of labor and P is a weighted average of p and e. The balance of trade is

$$\begin{aligned} BT &= pX^d(p, e) - eM \\ &= pX^d(p, e) - e(D_m(p, e, Z') \\ &\quad + G_m - Y_m^s(L_m^d(w/e)) \end{aligned} \tag{7.6}$$

where M is import, D_m is private demand for the importable good and G_m is government demand for the importable good.

In repressed inflation situations there is excess demand for both labor and the exportables output. Cuddington considered that total employment equals notional labor supply,

$$L = L^s(w/p, W/P) < L_x^d(w/p) + L_m^d(w/e). \qquad (7.7)$$

This is possible only when domestic households do not face a constraint in exportable good market where excess demand prevails and there is no need for a dual decision on the supply of labor. For this purpose Cuddington, unlike in the case of Kemp [13], assumed that domestic demands must be satisfied before the demands of foreigners when there is an excess world demand for the exportable good. He justified this assumption on the basis of the lower transport, transactions, queuing, and information costs faced by domestic residents and government export controls which guarantee that domestic output is rationed in a way to give preference to domestic demanders over foreigners.

Since labor is in short supply, some rationing scheme must evolve to allocate the available labor L among firms in the two industries. Although Cuddington argued that a rationing rule derived from the optimizing behavior of economic agents would be ideal, but is beyond the scope of his present research, the rationing rule proposed by him is quite interesting and useful, in view of the present stage of fix-price general equilibrium theory. The amount of labor allocated to each sector is given as

$$L_x^r = L_x^r(p, e, w, W), \qquad L_m^r = L_m^r(p, e, w, W) \qquad (7.8)$$

since total labor supply L^s is a function of w, W and P which is a weighted average of p and e. It is assumed that L_x^r is increasing with respect to p and decreasing with respect to e, and L_m^r is increasing with respect to e and decreasing with respect to p. Although laborers have no direct wage incentive to relocate when prices change, firms in the industry whose price rises will receive increased profits which can be used to attract workers by increasing advertising, job security or fringe benefits.

Nominal GNP in this case is

$$Y'' = pY_x^s(L_x^r(p, e, w, W)) + eY_m^s(L_m^r(p, e, w, W)) \qquad (7.9)$$

and exportables production falls short of total demand,

$$Y_x'' = Y_x^s(L_x^r(p, e, w, W)) < D_x(p, e, Z'') + G_x + X^d(p, e) \quad (7.10)$$

where $Z'' = Z''(Y'' - T, W)$. Since domestic demand is assumed to be met, foreigners do not receive all of the domestic exportables they demand and exports are restricted to

$$X''(p, e) = Y_x^s(L_x^r(p, e, w, W)) - D_x(p, e, Z'') - G_x. \quad (7.11)$$

The trade balance under repressed inflation equals

$$BT = pX'' - eM = (Y'' - T) - Z''(Y'' - T, W) - (pG_x + eG_m - T), \quad (7.12)$$

where T is the tax revenue of the government.

Cuddington [7] thus introduced the possibility of quantity constraints or rationing in the traded good market but he did it by giving up the traditional assumption of a small country. The implication of this is more fully explained in Cuddington [8] which considered a fix-price model with import quotas and excess demands in the domestic market for importables and yielded the interesting second best result that import quotas with importables price controls reduce the effectiveness on the balance of trade of exchange rate devaluation under Keynesian unemployment.

According to Cuddington [8], two situations are relevant to the problem whether the price of the exportables is fixed in terms of domestic or foreign currency. Firstly, the domestic economy is assumed to be able to affect the terms of trade, i.e., the foreign currency price of exportables relative to importables. This is likely if the domestic exportables are a differentiated product or if the country is a large supplier relative to the size of the world market. In this case, it is reasonable to assume that it is the price in terms of the domestic currency that is fixed in the short run. Keynesian unemployment is possible only in this case. The second case is where the foreign currency price of the exportables rather than the domestic currency price is fixed. This occurs when the domestic economy is small so that it faces a perfectly elastic demand for exportables at the foreign currency price.

It seems, therefore, that according to Cuddington quantity constraints in the market for exportables are faced by suppliers only when they are confronted with downward sloping demand curves, i.e., only in the case of monopoly or monopolistic competition. Otherwise, i.e., if each supplier is a small price taker, there cannot be a quantity constraint and Keynesian unemployment in Cuddington's model, even if the country itself is large so that she can affect the terms of trade by the joint action of all of her suppliers. But, as Leijonhufvud [62] emphasized, Keynes was adamantly opposed to theories that blamed depressions on such obstacles to price adjustments as monopolies, labor unions, minimum wage laws or other institutional constraints. And the quantity constraint model or fix-price theory as such does not necessarily presuppose that each supplier is not a price taker, as in the case of closed economy or in the case of non-traded good, although the primary criticism of fix-price models in general is that they fail to provide a rigorous theoretical justification of why prices and wages are sticky (Cuddington [8]). The problem left still unsolved is whether quantity constraints are faced by suppliers in the market for traded goods, even with the assumption of a small country or the assumption that each supplier is a small price taker. If a price taking supplier faces quantity constraints in a closed economy or in the non-traded good market, then there is no reason why it should not face them in the traded good market.

Bruno [5] also gave up the small country assumption partly in his consideration of the problem of import competition, which skillfully used a quantity constraint model and offered an interesting interpretation of structural problems in the 1970s. The question is why import competition which itself is nothing new has received so much attention in recent years. At times of rapid growth and excess demand in both the goods and labor markets, such as the late 1960s and early 1970s, import competition could alleviate shortages and reduce inflationary pressure. But, during a period of persistent slack as after 1973, it may compound existing adjustment problems. Bruno assumes that the country is small in the market for importables but not so in the market for the exportables. A home good is an imperfect substitute for a foreign good and the level of its export is a decreasing function of their relative price. Though the home country can thus in principle influence its terms of trade, however, all prices are fixed and the terms of trade do not change endogenously even in response to an excess supply of exports. As

Neary [70] rightly pointed out, therefore, the implication would be unaffected if the small country assumption is retained and the export demand function is replaced by an exogenous export sales constraint.

7.2. The role of exporters and importers

In both the neo-classical and traditional Keynesian theories of international trade, the price of a traded good is given in terms of foreign currency and changes in terms of domestic currency as the rate of exchange is changed, if the country is small and suppliers are price takers.[24] This is because of the assumption that domestic consumers can, if they wish, buy directly from foreign producers in the foreign market. This assumption may not be so unrealistic in international trade among countries, like European ones, closely located and socially and culturally very similar to each other. In international trade between countries far away and dissimilar, say US and Japan, however, the role of consumers is very limited and international trade is carried out almost exclusively by specialized firms, i.e., exporters and importers. Domestic consumers buy the importables in domestic market from foreign exporters or domestic importers, because consumers have neither enough information nor suitable credits to buy directly from foreign producers, cannot finance transportation cost individually and are not accustomed to foreign exchange business.

Negishi [20] considered a Keynesian situation where unlike in a Walrasian situation information is essentially imperfect, and demonstrated that the prices in terms of domestic currency both of a importables and of exportables are sticky in the face of a changing rate of exchange, if the domestic consumers have to buy the importables exclusively from the domestic importers and/or foreign exporters and the foreign consumers have to buy their importables exclusively from the foreign importers and/or domestic exporters. The domestic and foreign markets are considered separate and related only by the activities of domestic and foreign exporters and importers. In the domestic market for importables, suppliers are

---

[24] See, however, Cuddington [8] for the possibility of violation of the law of one price.

domestic import competing producers, domestic importers and foreign exporters, and all of them are assumed to take price as given in domestic currency and constrained by the limited demand, i.e., the existence of excess supply. Foreign import competing producers, domestic exporters and foreign importers are assumed to be in a similar situation in the foreign market for their importables.

These suppliers facing limited demand are assumed to perceive Sweezy type kinked demand curves, even though they are perfectly competitive. Unlike in the case of oligopoly, where the kink stems from the asymmetric behavior of rival firms, however, the kink is explained by the asymmetric behavior of customers due to imperfect information (Scitovsky [79], Negishi [72, pp. 36, 87], Stiglitz [84], and Reid [76, pp. 96–99]). A firm cannot expect a large increase in demand by reducing its price since customers currently buying from other firms are not perfectly informed. It has to expect, on the other hand, a large reduction of demand when it raises the price since customers currently buying from it are fully informed of the price rise and will quickly shift to other firms charging unchanged prices. If short term expectations are realized, the profit is maximized at the current level of sales, i.e., the constraint of the demand, where the demand curve is kinked. At this level the marginal revenue is discontinuous and the marginal cost curve passes between two separate parts of the marginal revenue curve. As was explained by Sweezy [86], it is then very likely that the price remains unchanged if the level of effective demand is changed or if the marginal cost curve is shifted. Though limited to the case of Keynesian unemployment, this provides a theoretical justification of why prices and wages are sticky (Cuddington [8], Negishi [72]).

An effect of the introduction of exporters and importers facing kinked demand curves into the Keynesian model of international trade is the possible rigidity of the price in domestic currency of the importables of a small country in the face of changing rate of exchange, since shifts in the marginal cost curves of domestic importers and foreign exporters are very likely to keep the price of importables charged to domestic consumers unchanged. A changing rate of exchange can affect the economy merely through the income effects which are due to foreign exchange gains and losses accrued to exporters and importers. These gains and losses arise from the fact that domestic exporters buy at the price given in terms of home currency and sell at the price given in terms of foreign currency, and domestic importers buy at the price given in terms of foreign currency and sell at the price given in terms of home currency.

Such an absence of changes in consumers' price is, of course, a short run phenomenon. In the long run foreign exchange gains induce the entry of new firms into profitable sectors. New entering firms have to undersell old existing firms so that prices charged to consumers are reduced in such sectors. In the short run, however, the domestic price of the importables is sticky in the face of a changing rate of exchange and, as our recent experiences show, the foreign exchange gains and losses mainly accrue not to the domestic consumers but to exporters and importers. Income effects of changes in the exchange rate are dominant over price and substitution effects. The stability of foreign exchange depends, then, not on the price elasticities of import demands which are essential for the stability in the traditional Keynesian model without exporters and importers (Kemp [57, p. 286]) but on propensities to consume and on whether international trades are carried out by domestic or foreign exporters or importers, i.e., whether foreign exchange gains and losses accrue to the exporting or importing country.

Suppose, for example, that international trade between two countries is exclusively carried out by the exporters and importers of a country, say the home country, so that both foreign exchange gains and losses accrue entirely to the home country. The relation between the level of output of the home country X and the level of national income of the home country x is given as

$$x = X + (R - 1)M^*(x^*) + (1 - R)M(x) \qquad (7.13)$$

where R is the rate of exchange defined as the price of foreign currency in terms of home currency which is equal to 1 initially, M and M^* are respectively home and foreign demand for import, and x^* is the level of national income of the foreign country. The second term on the right hand side of (7.13) signifies foreign exchange gains (when $R > 1$) and losses (when $R < 1$) of exporters and the third term signifies those of importers.

The level of output of the home country X and that of the foreign country x^*, which is identical to the level of the national income, are determined in the Keynesian model by the level of effective demand, i.e.,

$$X = D(x) + M^*(x^*) \tag{7.14}$$

and

$$x = D^*(x^*) + M(x) \tag{7.15}$$

where D and D^* are respectively the domestic demand for domestic goods of home and foreign countries.[25] By substituting (7.13) into (7.14) and (7.15) and differentiating by R, we have at $R = 1$,

$$dx/dR = (M - M^*)(1 - D^{*\prime})/A \tag{7.16}$$

and

$$dx^*/dR = (M - M^*)M'/A \tag{7.17}$$

where

$$A = (1 - D^{*\prime})(D' - 1) + M'M^{*\prime} \tag{7.18}$$

and D' is the derivative of D with respect to x and the like. A is negative if we assume that the marginal propensities to consume are less than one, i.e., $D' + M' < 1$ and $D^{*\prime} + M^{*\prime} < 1$.

The balance of trade of the home country in terms of foreign currency is $B = M^* - M$, since both what the home country received for M^* and what she pays for M are given in terms of foreign currency. The change in M due to a change in R is from (7.16) and (7.17)

$$dB/dR = (M - M^*)M'(D^{*\prime} + M^{*\prime} - 1)/A. \tag{7.19}$$

Suppose the home country's balance of trade is in surplus, i.e., $B > 0$, and the stock of foreign assets held by domestic residents increases. The condition for monetary equilibrium in the foreign exchange market requires that the domestic currency appreciates, i.e., R is reduced. Since $dB/dR < 0$ in (7.19), however, the appreciation of the home currency increases the trade surplus further, which implies the instability of the foreign exchange market

---

[25] The home country is assumed to be a large country, though all the suppliers are price takers facing demand constraints (perceiving kinked demand curves which are partially infinitely elastic). In the case of a small country (7.15) is deleted and x^* is considered constant, but the results are similar.

(Krueger [60, pp. 105–10]). The trade surplus and appreciation of her currency of a country actively participating in international trade (like Japan?) in the sense of foreign exchange risk bearing tends to destabilize the foreign exchange market since the stabilizing effect of the foreign exchange gains of her importers in increasing imports is overtaken by the destabilizing effect of foreign exchange losses of her exporters in decreasing imports.

7.3. Conclusion—problems solved and unsolved

Certainly it cannot be denied that quantity constraint models are useful to analyze some disequilibrium problems in international trade which the traditional equilibrium models cannot deal with adequately. The applications of quantity constraint models to international trade generate, however, new problems more often than they solve old ones.

We have seen that some have difficulty in dealing with the traditional assumption of a small country in the application of quantity constraint models. It should be emphasized that quantity constraints are not necessarily inconsistent with the small country assumption. In other words, as Neary [70] rightly pointed out, "there are two distinct dimensions to the usual assumption of a small open economy: first, world prices of traded goods are fixed, and second, it is possible to buy or sell an infinite amount at these prices, i.e., there are no export sales or import supply constraints."

Perhaps one reason for this difficulty is the fact that fixprice is simply assumed and not well explained in most of the theories of quantity constraints. Of course, some tried to explain it by using kinked demand curves. Others simply argued that the speed of adjustment is much slower for prices than for quantities. We must admit, however, that we have not yet had the standard theory which provided a satisfactory choice-theoretic basis for the assumption of fixprice in quantity constraint models.

Those who explained fixprice assumption are agreed that it is a temporary or short-run phenomenon (Bruno [5], Malinvaud [64, p. 12], Negishi [20])[26] and that prices may change in the medium run.

---

[26] Since changes in inventory are assumed away in most quantity constraint models, fix-price equilibrium can be conceived only if expectations are realized, which implies that the problem has to be of short term in the sense of Keynes [58].

If so, the application of fixprice quantity constraint models is useful, for example, in the problem of determining the short-run effects on output and employment of changes in the rate of exchange. If one wishes to explain, as Malinvaud [15], Dixit [9], Neary [18] did, the effects of technological progress, however, it is desirable either to explain fixprice in the longer run or to use medium-term models that admit induced changes in prices and wages.

Finally, we have to point out that considerations of exchange rate determination are often very old fashioned in the applications of quantity constraint models.[27] Rates of exchange are given exogenously and changed parametrically, which is appropriate for fix-exchange-rate system of the 1960s but not for the flexible-exchange-rate system which prevailed after 1973. The rate of exchange should be considered to be determined endogenously in models that allow interactions between the current account and the capital account.

References

1. Basic References

[1] Benassy, J. P., "A Neo-Keynesian Model of Price and Quantity Determination in Disequilibrium," G. Schwödiauer, ed., *Equilibrium and Disequilibrium in Economic Theory*, D. Reidel 1977, 511–544.

[2] Brecher, R., "Optimal Commercial Policy for a Minimum-Wage Economy," *Journal of International Economics*, 1974.

[3] Brecher, R., "Minimum Wage Rates and the Pure Theory of International Trade." *Quarterly Journal of Economics 88*, no. 1 (1974), 98–116.

[4] Brito, D. L. and J. D. Richardoson, "Some Disequilibrium Dynamics of Exchange Rate Changes," *Journal of International Economics, 5* (1975), 1–13.

[5] Bruno, M., "Import Competition and Macroeconomic Adjustment under Wage-Price Rigidity," in *Import Competition and Response* ed. by J. Bhagwati. Chicago: University of Chicago Press, 1982, 11–32.

[6] Chan, K. S., "The Employment Effects of Tariffs under a Free Exchange Rate Regime," *Journal of International Economics, 8* (1978), 415–423.

[7] Cuddington, J. T., "Fisical and Exchange Rate Policies in a Fix-Price Trade Model With Export Rationing," *Journal of International Economics, 10* (1980), 319–340.

[8] Cuddington, J. T., "Import Substitution Policies: A Two-Sector, Fix-Price Model," *Review of Economic Studies, 48* (1981), 327–342.

[9] Dixit, A., "The Balance of Trade in a Model of Temporary Equilibrium with Rationing," *Review of Economic Studies, 45* (1978), 393–404.

---

[27] A recent exception is, however, Cuddington–Johansson–Lofgren [36, chapters 5 and 7].

[10] Haberler, G., "Some Problems in the Pure Theory of International Trade." *Economic Journal 60,* no. **238** (1950): 223–240.

[11] Hahn, F. H., "The Monetary Approach to the Balance of Payments," *Journal of International Economics,* **7** (1977), 231–249.

[12] Harberger, A. C., "Currency Depreciation, Income, and the Balance of Trade," *Journal of Political Economy,* **58** (1950), 47–60.

[13] Kemp, M. C., "Depreciation in Disequilibrium," *Canadian Journal of Economics and Political Science,* **25** (1959), 431–438.

[14] Liviatan, N., "A Disequilibrium Analysis of the Monetary Trade Model," *Journal of International Economics,* **9** (1979), 355–377.

[15] Malinvaud, E., *The Theory of Unemployment Reconsidered,* Blackwell, 1977, 1985.

[16] Meade, J. E., The Balance of Payments, *Mathematical Supplement,* Oxford University Press, 1951.

[17] Michaely, M., "Domestic Effects of Devaluation under Repressed Inflation," *Journal of Political Economy,* **63** (1955), 512–524.

[18] Neary, J. P., "Nontraded Goods and the Balance of Trade in a Neo-Keynesian Temporary Equilibrium," *Quarterly Journal of Economics,* **95** (1980), 403–429.

[19] Neary, J. P., "Intersectoral Capital Mobility, Wage Stickiness, and the Case for Adjustment Assistance," *Import Competition and Response,* ed. by J. Bhagwati. Chicago: University of Chicago Press, 1982, 39–67.

[20] Negishi, T., "Foreign Exchange Gains in a Keynesian Model of International Trade," *Economie Appliquée,* **32** (1979b), 623–633.

2. Other References

[21] Baldwin, R. E., "Equilibrium in International Trade: A Diagrammatic Analysis." *Quarterly Journal of Economics 62,* no. 4 (1948): 748–762.

[22] Barro, R. J., and H. I. Grossman, "A General Disequilibrium Model of Income and Employment," *American Economic Review,* **61** (1971), 82–93.

[23] Barro, R. J., and H. I. Grossman: *Money, Employment and Inflation,* Cambridge University Press (1976).

[24] Benassy, J. P., "Neo-Keynesian Disequilibrium in a Monetary Economy," *Review of Economic Studies,* **42** (1975), 503–523.

[25] Bhagwati, J., "Immiserizing Growth: A Geometric Note," *Review of Economic Studies,* 1958.

[26] Bhagwtai, H. N. and T. N. Srinivasan, "Optimal Intervention to Achieve Noneconomic Objectives," *Review of Economic Studies,* **36** (1969), 27–38.

[27] Bhagwati, J., "The Generalized Theory of Distortions and Welfare." In *Trade, Balance of Payments, and Growth: Paper in International Economics in Honor of Charles P. Kindleberger,* 1971. Chapter 12.

[28] Bhagwati, J. N., and T. N. Srinivasan, "On Reanalyzing the Harris–Todaro Model: Policy ranking in the Case of Sector-Specific Sticky Wages." *American Economic Review,* 1974.

[29] Bhagwati, J. N., *Lectures on International Trade.* Cambridge, Mass., The MIT Press, 1983.

[30] Bhagwati, J. N., R. A. Brecher, and T. Hatta, "The Generalized Theory of Transfers and Welfare: Bilateral Transfers in a Multilateral World," *The American Economic Review,* September 1983, 606–618.

[31] Brecher, R. and Bhagwati, Jugdish., "Immiserizing Transfers from Abroad," *Journal of International Economics,* November 1982, **13**, 353–64.

[32] Brecher, R. and C. Diaz-Alejandro, "Tariffs, Foreign Capital and Immiserizing Growth," *Journal of International Economics,* **7** (1977), 317–322.

[33] Caves, R. E. and R. W. Jones, *World Trade and Payments*. Boston: Little, Brown and Company, 1981.

[34] Chipman, J. S., "A Survey of the Theory of International Trade: Part 1, The Classical Theory," *Econometrica* 33, no. **3** (1965), 477–519.

[35] Clower, R. W., "The Keynesian Counter-Revolution: A Theoretical Appraisal," F. H. Hahn and F. P. R. Brechling, eds., *The Theory of Interest*, Macmillan, 1965, 103–125.

[36] Cuddington, J. T., P. O. Johansson and K. G. Lofgren, *Disequilibrium Macroeconomics in Open Economies*, Basil Blackwell, 1984.

[37] Das, S. P., "Effects of Foreign Investment in the Presence of Unemployment," *Journal of International Economics*, **11** (1981), 249–257.

[38] Das, S. P., "On the Effect of Tariff on Employment under Flexible Exchange Rate," *Journal of International Economics*, **12** (1982), 165–168.

[39] Dixit, A., and V. Norman, *Theory of International Trade*, Cambridge Unversity Press, 1980. Chapter 9.

[40] Dixit, A., Comment on "Capital Mobility, Wage Stickiness, and Adjustment Assistance (by J. P. Neary)" in *Import Competition and Response*, ed. by J. N. Bhagwati. Chicago: University of Chicago Press, 1982.

[41] Emmanuel, A., Unequal Exchange, B. Pearce tr., Monthly Review Press, 1972.

[42] Frenkel, J. A. and H. C. Johnson, eds., *The Monetary Approach to the Balance of Payments*, George Allen and Unwin (1976).

[43] Graaff, J., "On Optimum Tariff Structures," *Review of Economic Studies*, 17, no. **42** (1949–50), 47–59.

[44] Harris, John R. and Michael P. Todaro, "Migration, Unemployment and Development: A Two-Sector Analysis." *American Economic Review* 60, no. **1** (1970): 126–142.

[45] Helpman, E., "Macroeconomic Policy in a Model of International Trade with a Wage Restriction," *International Economic Review*, **17** (1976), 262–277.

[46] Helpman, E., "Nontraded Goods and Macroeconomic Policy under a Fixed exchange rate," Quarterly Journal of Economics, **91** (1977), 469–480.

[47] Hicks, J., *Capital and Growth*, Oxford University Press, 1965.

[48] Hildenbrand, J. and W. Hildenbrand, "On Keynesian Equilibria with Unemployment and Quantity Rationing," *Journal of Economic Theory*, **18** (1978), 5–277.

[49] Hillman, A. L., "Unilateral and Bilateral Trade Policies for a Minimum-Wage Economy," *Journal of International Economics*, **11** (1981), 407–413.

[50] Ito, T., "An Example of a Non-Walrasian Equilibrium with Stochastic Rationing at the Walrasian Equilibrium Prices," *Economic Letters*, **2** (1979), 13–19.

[51] Johansson, P. O. and K. G. Lofgren, "The Effects of Tariffs and Real Wages on Employment in a Barro–Grossman Model of an Open Economy," *Scandinavian Journal of Economics*, **82** (1980), 167–183.

[52] Johansson, P. O. and K. G. Lofgren, "A Note on Employment Effects of Tariffs in a Small Open Economy," *Weltwirtschaftliches Archiv*, **117** (1981), 578–583.

[53] Johnson, Harry G., "Income Distribution, the Offer Curve and the Effects of Tariffs," *Manchester School of Economics*, September 1960, **28** 223–42.

[54] Johnson, H. G., "The Possibility of Income Losses from Increased Efficiency or Factor Accumulation in the Presence of Tariffs," *Economic Journal*, 1967.

[55] Johnson, H. G., "Minimum Wage Laws: A General Equilibrium Analysis." *Canadian Journal of Economics* 2, no. **4** (1969): 599–604.

[56] Jones, R. W., "A Three-Factor Model in Theory, Trade and History." In *Trade, Balance of Payments, and Growth: Papers in International Economics in Honor of Charles P. Kindleberger*, ed. J. N. Bhagwati *et al.* (Amsterdam: North-Holland, 1971), 3–21.

[57] Kemp, M. C., *The Pure Theory of International Trade*, Prentice-Hall, 1964.

[58] Keynes, J. M., *The General Theory of Employment, Interest and Money*, Macmillan, 1936.

[59] Komiya, R. and T. Suzuki, "Transfer Payments and Income Distribution," *Manchester School of Economics* **35** September 1967, 245–55.

[60] Krueger, A. O., *Exchange-Rate Determination*, Cambridge University Press, 1983.

[61] Lefeber, L., "Trade and Minimum Wage Rates." In *Trade, Balance of Payments, and Growth: Papers in International Economics in Honor of P. Kindleberger*, ed. J. Bhagwati *et al.* (Amsterdam: North-Holland, 1971), 91–114.

[62] Leijonhufvud, A, "Keynes and the Keynesians: A Suggested Interpretation," *American Economic Review*, **57** (1967), 401–410.

[63] Machlup, F., *International Trade and the National Income Multiplier*, Philadelphia, Blackiston, 1943.

[64] Malinvaud, E., *Profitability and Unemployment*, Cambridge University Press, 1980.

[65] Mayer, W, "Short-run and Long-run Equilibrium for a Small Open Economy." *Journal of Political Economy 82*, no. **4** (1974): 955–967.

[66] Muellbauer, J. and R. Portes, "Macroeconomic Models with Quantity Rationing," *Economic Journal*, **88** (1978), 393–404.

[67] Mundell, R. A., *International Economics*. Macmillan, 1968.

[68] Mussa, M., "Tariffs and the Distribution of Income: The Importance of Factor Specificity, Substitutability, and Intensity in the Short and Long Run." *Journal of Political Economy 82*, no. **5** (1974), 1191–1203.

[69] Mussa, M., "The-Sector Model in Terms of Its Dual: A Geometric Exposition." *Journal of International Economics*, 1979.

[70] Neary, J. P., *Comment* (on Bruno (1982)), in *Import Competition and Response*, ed. by J. Bhagwati, University of Chicago Press, 1982, 32–37.

[71] Neary, J. P., "International Factor Mobility, Minimum Wage Rates and Factor-Price Equalization: A Synthesis," forthcoming *Quarterly Journal of Economics*.

[72] Negishi, T., *Microeconomic Foundations of Keynesian Macroeconomics*, North-Holland Publishing Co, 1979a.

[73] Negishi, T., "From Samuelson's Stability Analysis to Non-Walrasian Economics," G. R. Feiwel, ed., *Samuelson and Neoclassical Economics*, Kluwer-Nijhoff Publishing, 1982, s19–125.

[74] Norman, K. and R. W. Jones, "A Model of Trade and Unemployment," in *General Equilibrium, Growth and Trade: Essays in Honor of Lionel W. McKenzie*, eds. by Green, J.R. and J. A. Scheinkman. New York: Academic press, 1979.

[75] Patinkin, D., *Money, Interest and Prices*, Harper and Row, 1964.

[76] Reid, G. C., *The Kinked Demand Curve Analysis of Oligopoly*, Edinburgh University Press, 1981.

[77] Samuelson, P. A., *Foundations of Economic Analysis*, Harvard University Press, 1947.

[78] Samuelson, P. A., "Maximum Principles in Analytical Economics," *American Economic Review*, **62** (1972), 249–263.

[79] Scitovsky, T., "Asymmetries in Economics," *Scottish Journal of Political Economy* **25** (1978), 227–237.

[80] Shapiro, C. and J. E. Stighitz, "Equilibrium Unemployment as a Worker Discipline Device," *American Economic Review,* **74** (No. 2) (1984), 433–444.

[81] Srinivasan, T. N. and J. N. Bhagwati,, "Alternative Policy Ranking in a Large Open Economy with Sector-Specific Minimum Wages." *Journal of Economic Theory,* 1975.

[82] Steedman, I., Ed., *Fundamental Issues in Trade Theory,* Macmillan, 1979.

[83] Steigum, E., "Keynesian and Classical Unemployment in an Open Economy," *Scandinavian Journal of Economics* **82** (1980), 147–166.

[84] Stiglitz, J. E., "Equilibrium in Product Markets with Imperfect Information," *American Economic Review,* **69** (1979), 338–345.

[85] Swan, T. W., "Longer-run Problems of the Balance of Payments," H. W. Arndt and W. M. Corden, eds., *The Australian Economy,* Cheshire Press, 1963.

[86] Sweezy, P. M., "Demand under Conditions of Oligopoly," *Journal of Political Economy,* **47** (1939), 568–573.

[87] Tsiang, S. C., "The Role of Money in Trade-Balance Stability: Synthesis of the Elasticity and Absorption Approaches." *American Economic Review,* **51** (1961), 912–936.

[88] Varian, H. R., *Microeconomic Analysis,* Norton, 1978.

[89] Weiss, A., "Job Queues and Layoffs in Labor Markets with Flexible Wages," *Journal of Political Economy,* **88** (1980), 526–38.

[90] Yano, M., "Welfare Aspects in Transfer Problem: On the Validity of the 'Neo-Orthodox' Presumptions," *Journal of International Economics,* **15** (1983), 277–289.

[91] Yellen, J. L., "Efficiency Wage Models of Unemployment," *American Economic Review,* **74** (No. 2) (1984), 200–5.

INDEX

FUNDAMENTALS OF PURE AND APPLIED ECONOMICS

Additional volumes in preparation
ISSN: 0191-1708